QUMRAN COMMUNITY

CIRCA 100 B.C.

Copyright Time Inc. 1957
TIME Map by R. M. Chapin, Jr.

THE DEAD SEA SCROLLS
AND THE LIVING CHURCH

CARL G. HOWIE

the Dead Sea Scrolls and the Living Church

JOHN KNOX PRESS
RICHMOND, VIRGINIA

Dedicated to
Frank M. Cross, Jr.
Scholar and Friend
in appreciation of his work
on the Dead Sea Scrolls

Foreword

ARCHAEOLOGY TO MANY has suggested the labors of
eccentric scholars who spend their lives excavating in areas
of the world long ago deserted by men who struck their tents
and moved to greener pastures. Most of us are concerned
about today—and even more about the day after today—than
about the lives of peasants and potentates of lost civilizations.
That the discovery of what are known as the Dead Sea Scrolls
should have roused such widespread interest among both
Christians and the opponents of Christianity raises significant
questions.

Books on the Scrolls have been numbered among the best-
sellers. Is this because the Scrolls involve not simply the discovery of a dead culture but also a challenge to the living
faith men are trying so desperately to find and which they
thought they had possessed, at least in part? The final authen-
tication of the Christian faith suddenly faced yet another
crisis based upon scientific discoveries. For some the foundation of the Church no longer was that unshakable rock but
had turned to the sand that covered the Scrolls. Was Jesus
after all simply another devotee of a religious community?
Were the "silent years" (from the age of twelve until His
baptism by John) spent by Jesus as a member of the desert

7

community of the Essenes? Were His teachings and pattern of life directly inspired by a unique relationship with God, or did His life simply result from the daily discipline and thinking He had learned with other members of the Essene community at the Qumran Plateau? If the Essene community was responsible, wherein lies the uniqueness of Jesus or of the Christian faith?

In past ages the Church as an institution has known periods of falling away from faith when spiritual apathy and even corruption have despoiled the garments of the Bride of Christ; nevertheless, the Church by the indwelling of God's Spirit has always found the secret of reforming zeal and power. But if the Bridegroom be found to be less than the Bridegroom—merely a spiritual genius among somewhat less spiritual men—where then is faith? Precisely such a challenge to faith has been made by the embalming sands in their miraculous preservation of documents of the Essene community written in the contemporary language of Our Lord's day and outlining in detail a life of high and noble spiritual discipline.

Dr. Howie's book arrives at an opportune time. The translations of the Scrolls have been made available to the public. The extreme darkness of pessimistic doubt has been dispelled; but an understandable twilight of doubt still remains in the minds of some Christians. We must now see the Scrolls more objectively, recognizing afresh the value of this most important single archaeological discovery in the area of Biblical scholarship. Dr. Howie has made available to us in small compass the exciting facts uncovered in the discovery. He has also provided that historical setting without which the text of the Scrolls can have no historical significance. He has brought

his own gifted mind to bear upon the Scrolls and by objective
and scholarly commentary has faced fearlessly many questions with which the less informed Christian has had to deal.

But he has done much more. Dr. Howie has made it possible for many to achieve the faith which they thought they
had lost but really had never possessed at all. Pious familiar-
ity with the "old, old story of Jesus and His love," particularly
among Christians nurtured at mother's knee and in mother
church, often can lead to an acquiescent indifference to the
unique and challenging nature of the Good News of God.
The Qumran discoveries have sent many of us back to re-
assess the things we thought we "most surely believed." The
Scrolls taken in conjunction with the Gospels portray the
figure of Our Lord as larger than ever, towering over even
this dedicated community of Essenes.

GEORGE M. DOCHERTY

The New York Avenue Presbyterian Church
Washington, D. C.

Preface

As a pastor in Washington, D. C., where the local newspapers reported extensively on the discovery and interpretation of the Dead Sea Scrolls, I found the news to be very disturbing and misleading to the majority of church people. Appearance of new works on the subject did not seem to dispel the misapprehension, perhaps because some authors had an "axe to grind," some volumes were not written in an understandable style, and certain valuable discussions were very difficult to get. One man who was a member of the congregation in Washington asked in all seriousness, "Does this discovery mean that Christians now must give up their faith?" Of course there were others who felt that the evidence had no bearing on the origins of New Testament faith and life. As a result of these experiences a decision was reached to add one more volume to the long list of titles on the Dead Sea Scrolls in the hope that some misapprehensions might be set at rest by bringing the evidence in perspective.

This volume was made possible because many individuals were most helpful with their suggestions for improvement. Written during the summer of 1956 at the American Schools of Oriental Research, the manuscript was read by Frank Cross, Jr., by Paul Leslie Garber, and by Bernard Boyd. Their

11

suggestions and corrections have become a part of the book. To them, especially to Dr. Cross, the author is most indebted. Typing of the first draft was done by Mrs. Neil Richardson in Jerusalem. The second draft was copied by Mrs. Madeline Adams and the final manuscript was finished by my wife, Jean Howie. Their skillful work is acknowledged here with gratitude. Finally our thanks go to Misses Margaret Petsch and Jane Dachtelberg for their editorial suggestions which made the manuscript more readable. With this recognition of indebtedness to many, the writer presents the volume to those who wish to know what the relationship of the Dead Sea Scrolls is to the Living Church. He recognizes that this is a partial and tentative answer.

CARL G. HOWIE

San Francisco

Contents

1. the Desert Speaks

THE DESERT has always protected her secrets by forbidding men to dwell in her domain and by appearing to possess nothing of any value. Sand, heat, and perpetual drought discourage not only human intruders but even some insects from seeking habitation therein. Yet this condition, the absence of living organisms and the inaccessibility to marauders, makes the arid land a place of safety for treasures left there by the passing pageant of history.

For centuries that area of Palestine west of the Jordan, about seven miles south of steaming, subtropical Jericho, gave promise of nothing but trouble for those who dared profane it. It was assumed that the parched and windswept plateaus of the region, protected on all sides by mountains, desert, or the sea, had always been an uninhabited area but for an occasional military encampment insignificant for the history of man and his faith. Except for Bedouins, only the mystic or recluse found here a place of retreat, but his eyes were not focused to see or to uncover the artifacts of the past.

For nineteen hundred years the desert succeeded in protecting "the best-kept secret of the ages." Only through the combined alchemy of circumstance and archaeological science did the barren region finally yield that secret. In 1947 a Bedouin, clambering up a rock-strewn cliff in search of a goat, discovered Cave I with its fabulous cache of seven relatively well-preserved and complete scrolls, together with numerous fragments of other literature. The story of the attempt to peddle these scrolls, first in the markets of Bethlehem and then in Jerusalem, has been told many times. Some were purchased by the Hebrew University in Jerusalem while others were brought to the United States by the Syrian archbishop, into whose hands they had come. Gradually but surely, through the study of this and large quantities of other material discovered later in the same region, haunting forms long forgotten rose to walk again in once familiar surroundings. Ideas silenced by the cruel, destructive power of untutored men have been revived and their content understood afresh. Influences long neglected are allowed to have their place in the scheme of things.

The interpretation of this material and the community which produced it is of special significance to Christians and Jews since the Qumran colony in the desert flourished during the lifetime of Jesus, which time was also a formative era in the history of Judaism. A real tempest has arisen in subsequent discussion about the origins of the Christian faith and Church in relationship to this particular Jewish sect. Opinions have ranged from one extreme to the other. Some claim that the materials have no bearing on the origins of the Christian movement, while others maintain that the Qumran community is an original of which Jesus Christ and the Christian faith are but copy. An investigation and assessment of the evidence for the layman should help to clarify some of the issues involved if indeed it cannot finally settle them.

In order to understand the manuscripts which have been discovered, the reader should know something about those who produced them. That desert settlement from whose inhabitants the scrolls came began during the middle part of the second century B.C. when a company of Jews, having turned its back on sinful society, migrated from the north to the Qumran plateau. Whether this "society apart" originated in Damascus, what its prior history and development in Israel had been, we can only surmise; but this much is sure —from the outset the movement was reactionary both in religious and in social attitude. Led at one point by a Teacher of Righteousness, who left his indelible imprint on the movement, this religious microcosm took root in the desert. According to the Jewish historian, Josephus, numerous parties of the same type existed in the first century A.D., inhabiting some villages as well as the Judaean and Jordan wildernesses.

Every sect or group, however small, is in some sense a product of the times in which it developed. That this isolated desert society might not be cut loose from the historical events and ideological tensions which produced it, a brief review of contemporary history is necessary. Setting the smaller picture in the larger framework of the times gives a basis for clearer historical perspective. This particular phase of the complex which is Judaism began to evolve, at least in its basic drives, with the Maccabean Revolt (about 165 B.C.), when the Hasidim ("holy ones") joined in Israel's historic struggle for liberty. That mortal conflict developed when the Seleucids, who were rulers in Syria-Mesopotamia, gained control of Palestine at the beginning of the second century and instituted a series of reforms looking toward assimilation of native culture to Greek ways.

It is important to remember that with the conquest of the Near East by Alexander the Great (336-323 B.C.), the whole area came within the orbit of Greek cultural influence. Alexander's death in 323 B.C. did not alter the ideological situation in that area since his successors were Greek generals who were complete devotees of Greek ways. The rule of the Ptolemies (dynasty established in Egypt by Ptolemy I, 323-283 B.C.) and Seleucids (dynasty established in Syria by Seleucus I, 312-280 B.C.) continued in the Near East until the intervention of Rome in Egypt and Syria (about 63 B.C.). Both Egypt and Syria became thoroughly Greek, and a clash between the new and the old seemed almost inevitable. Yet, that spiritual conflict did not commence until the notorious ruler Antiochus Epiphanes (175-163 B.C.) sought by direct action to force the Jews to conform to Greek ways and customs. Pigs, despised as unclean by Jews, were sacrificed in the Temple at Jerusalem, which had been rededicated to the Greek high god Zeus Olympus, while possession of the sacred Jewish Law of Moses was made a capital offense, as was the confirmatory rite of circumcision. Circumcision and the Law of Moses were the marks of separation between Jew and Greek. Remove the marks, so the Greeks reasoned, and the separation would be undone. But all Hebrews did not agree. Leading the dissent in its most violent form was a certain Mattathias, who served as priest in the little village of Modin. It was he who actually began a revolt which was led after his death by a son Judas, who was also called Maccabaeus. In honor of Judas' leadership the rebellion was thereafter called the Maccabean Revolt.

The tides of power and struggle finally favored the Maccabean cause although Judas himself died on the field of battle. His brothers who succeeded to the revolutionary leadership were able to finish Jewish liberation by a combination of force and diplomacy. Not long after this emancipation was accomplished by Judas and his brothers (Jonathan and Simon), the startling realization began to dawn on the revolutionaries that the substitution of such native rulers as John Hyrcanus (134-104 B.C.), Aristobulus I (104-103 B.C.), and Alexander Jannaeus (103-76 B.C.) was not an improvement over the rule of foreign conquerors. Indeed these three, like Jonathan and Simon before them, took for themselves not only the office of secular ruler but the position of High Priest as well. The "secular" Greek spirit which was resisted to the death during the Maccabean Revolt proved to be a resilient force that ultimately influenced men who still claimed to be, and thought they were, devout Jews. When the accommodation of the Hebrew religion to Greek attitudes and practices reached an advanced stage, with a resultant neglect of the faith by the heirs of the revolution, there arose a separatist movement whose members were called Pharisees.

The Greek spirit, which opposed the Hebrew faith, not only included the display of youth in scanty attire at athletic contests but also tended in general to corrupt the morals of young people. Even the Romans complained about the influences of Greek culture in their society, especially among the young. The intent of the Greeks was that the youth organization (*epheboi*), the political forum (*agora*), and the gymnasium should support an ideal of physical perfection and personal restraint, freeing the individual for worth-while intellectual pursuits. The Pharisees, however, did not recognize these ideals. In order to cope with this Greek threat to their traditional faith, they continued to live in society but protected themselves from encroachments of the world by "the fence of the Law," that is to say, by strict adherence to rules and regulations. Nevertheless, some of

the finer intellectual and aesthetic Greek influences remained.

Out of this general historical and ideological context the
Essene movement, which had adherents in many places, developed. At the outset it was possibly a conservative wing
of the Pharisees, but later there was complete disassociation
with that party of Judaism. The splintering of an original
reform, far from being unusual, is just what might be expected. Essenes observed the Law in a more stringent
manner than did the Pharisees. Moreover, at some point in
their history they refused to live as an integral part of the
social structure. Seeing what they thought was a corruption
of the morals and manners not only of society in general but
also of the Pharisees in particular, they chose to withdraw
from the world entirely. Several colonies were organized
throughout the region of Palestine. Some were located on
the edge of the desert; others were separated from the common life by other means. Each colony, similar in attitude,
had local peculiarities. For example, some colonies allowed
marriage; others possibly frowned on it. Some communities
forbade possession of private property while others permitted individual ownership. Whether all took the extreme
course of withdrawal which the Qumran community followed cannot be finally determined on the basis of available
evidence; perhaps some lived in the environs of various cities
and not in the desert, but all except those especially trained
and designated continued to avoid the contamination of society. In the early second century B.C. a company, forsaking a
world which it adjudged unworthy and sinful, retreated into
the desert and began to erect a home for the True Israel,
which they considered themselves to be! This band was,
according to its own interpretation, the purified Remnant of

whom the prophets had spoken. Although their departure from their former habitat was in all probability hastened by persecution both of their non-conformist party and its leader, the Teacher of Righteousness, a more important reason for choosing desert life was involved. Remembering the prophecy of Isaiah, this zealous segment of Judaism came into the desert to set the stage for prophetic fulfillment. Their *Manual of Discipline*, which was discovered in Cave I by Bedouins, explains the retreat in the following terms:

> and when these things shall come to pass to the Community in Israel according to these rules they shall separate themselves from the habitation of perverse men to go to the wilderness to clear there a way of Him as it is written
>
>> In the wilderness clear the way of . . .
>> Make straight in the desert the highway
>> for our God
>
> This (way) is the study of law (which) he commanded through Moses so that one might act according to all that was revealed time after time and according to that which the prophets have revealed through his Holy Spirit.[1]

Thus, the Qumran community moved into the desert, apart from the corrupting influence of society, to prepare the way for the Messianic Age. Preparation was accomplished through a strict devotion to the Law of God. Actually, only those who had joined the community were presumed to be capable of fulfilling the Law, thus hastening the advent of the Messianic Age. Since the Qumran holy society was *per se* True Israel and the Righteous Remnant, its members were especially anxious to establish conditions that would bring in the Age of the Messiah in which they were to be the chief beneficiaries.

Coming to the Qumran plateau, which is set like a shelf against the towering rocky cliffs of the mountains, the group discovered a place which can be best approached from the north through the desert. Cut off by the Dead Sea to the south and east, the way west is blocked by towering peaks over which goats and Bedouins travel only at the risk of life and limb. Isolated in this manner from the outside world the Essenes found for themselves a place where life was rather easy. Although it seldom rained on the plateau itself, water rushed down off the mountains during the annual rainy season and was trapped in cisterns and reservoirs at the foot of the cliffs. From these the water flowed down the gentle slope in a viaduct to the community center. At the community building it ran through a series of viaducts and channels which served to bring running water into practically all parts of the structure. This precious fluid, which was stored in huge cisterns, was used in a dozen or more baths, cisterns, or settling pools which have been recently unearthed. Water was the key to the physical and spiritual life of the Essene compound.

As one stands on the plateau and looks south he can see just below at the Dead Sea level a green coastal plain watered by a spring, Ain Feshka, which flows from the foot of the mountain. Several types of vegetation, including the tamarisk tree, still thrive on this plain where today's Bedouins leave their cattle for grazing and watering. Water from Ain Feshka is clear and pure when it comes from the ground and becomes brackish only after it has flowed closer to the Dead Sea. Here fruits and vegetables could easily have been grown in profusion once encroachment of the salt water was stopped. Because the weather is warm the year around, abundant harvests were possible according to the natural productivity of plants themselves. Food supply was, therefore, no problem; it is probable that the community was practically self-sufficient.

So far as animal husbandry is concerned, that also was made easy by the presence of Ain Feshka's life-giving water. Cattle, sheep, and goats could graze on the mountains during the rainy season, returning to the well-watered plain for the hot and dry season even as the Bedouins' cattle do today.

Ain Feshka's oasis-like plain was connected with the community center on the plateau, explaining clearly how life was sustained with sufficient food and drink. Buildings, the exact nature of which is still not certain, have been uncovered near Ain Feshka indicating that some part of Qumran life was centered there and not entirely on the plateau. Today one is amazed to come upon a pool more than fifty feet in diameter fed by waters from beneath the dry mountain. Certainly this second century B.C. band of desert wanderers, having come down the Jordan Valley from Damascus, was happily surprised by the sight of a spring in the desert and undoubtedly understood the discovery to be the result of God's guidance. Since it was impossible for them to move further south, they remained in this potential paradise, to which apparently the Almighty had brought them.

It can only be surmised what sort of activity engaged the hands of these holy men. In addition to agriculture and animal husbandry, weaving and pottery-making were necessary skills. However, no instruments of war were fashioned by these pacifists. Sandals were provided from shops in the main building, as were instruments of iron used in agricultural pursuits. It is probable that in addition to other ac-

tivities, the Essenes of necessity became rather adept build-
ers, making good use of material available in the desert.
Stone of a good quality and other materials could be collected there in abundance.

At the outset, a community edifice was erected out of
huge, roughly dressed stones, gathered from the immediate
area. Located on a peninsula-like promontory of a plateau
about one quarter the altitude of the background mountain
range, this building was the focal point for the life of the
sect but was in no sense living quarters for all members. It
may well be that there were other buildings in nearby areas
but this one served as a sort of community hub. (Recently
building remains have been found on the Ain Feshka plain.)
During the two main periods of occupation (about 125-31
B.C. and A.D. 6-68), the members of the community found
living quarters in booths or in tents which were pitched
around the center, much as earlier Hebrews had put their
tents and booths near the tabernacle. Some probably lived
in caves like those in which the scrolls were discovered, but
probably only a few did so. The central building, having two
stories at some points, was divided into a number of rooms
varying in size from mere cubicles to a spacious meeting
place or dining area. Measuring 118 feet by 94 feet, the
building was dominated on the northwest corner nearest to
the mountains by a tower which served the dual purpose of
lookout and defense. The walls were massive, very thick at
the base and becoming narrower as the height increased,
serving in effect as their own buttress. Without windows, the
tower's thick walls provided good protection for defenders
since in dire emergency it was possible to isolate it from the
rest of the building and thus hold out against the attack of
an enemy even if the remainder of the community center

were overrun. Located on a high plateau, the building in its crude way was an imposing structure, especially for the desert, where such construction was hardly common. Here in this isolated spot where even today the quietude is remarkable, the inhabitants focused their entire lives and in death were buried in a cemetery numbering now more than twelve hundred graves. The burial ground is located close by the structure in the direction of the Dead Sea shore. These graves, covered with rock, are a dramatic reminder that in another era men and women sought diligently in this place a better life of the spirit.

Within, on the first floor at the southwest corner, three large rooms and a small court accounted for a large part of the total floor space. Later excavations indicate that the center covered an even more extensive area. One room measured seventy feet in length. It was in this spacious place that the sect met for its two meals, and in this or an adjoining area the membership gathered for prayer and study of the Scriptures. Smaller rooms served as storage spaces, kitchens, pottery shops, and workrooms of every description. Some of these small rooms opened on the above-mentioned court, whose use is not known. On the second floor, above the main assembly room, there was a room furnished with a large plaster table sixteen feet long which provided writing space for scribes. Ink pots of bronze and pottery were a part of the equipment for the scribes, who reproduced the sacred Scriptures, made copies of commentaries, collected psalms, and provided an adequate number of rulebooks for the community. Plaster basins for ceremonial washing were kept in their "writing room" for those who copied this sacred law. On the southeast corner, in an area almost isolated from the rest of the building, were two pools which probably served as baths. The larger of the two occupied the major portion of the west wall. Fourteen steps leading down into the water were separated into four lanes by low walls at the top, as if to allow four individuals or groups to enter the water at the same time. Near it had been dug a round cistern with spiral stairs leading down to the water level. The citizens of Qumran used these pools of many sizes, shapes, and descriptions for daily baths, the nature of which will concern us later. An earthquake about 31 B.C. rendered the two original pools and the defense tower useless. The fault caused in the steps of one pool was at least six to eight inches. This community center was not occupied at the time of the catastrophe nor for some thirty-seven years afterward until the sect returned in A.D. 6 to reoccupy its home. At that time, a larger pool necessary to community life was constructed outside the main building to replace those destroyed in the earthquake. In the reconstruction period the center probably grew like Topsy, with necessity the key to expansion. Detailed description of other structural changes does not concern us for the purposes of this book, since some have yet to be published by the field archaeologists who are at work on the site.

As a member of the sect stood in the lookout tower he could have seen to the north the ghost-like hillocks of the Jordan wilderness giving way in the foreground to desert near the seaside. Jericho was hidden from view by the mountains but the Jordan as it emptied into the Dead Sea was clearly visible. To the west the watcher saw only the rocky cliffs of the mountains whose welcome shadow brought coolness across the plateau in the late afternoon. Across the sea in massive grandeur stood Mount Nebo. Southward was the Dead Sea, but before that the pleasant land of Ain Feshka lying several hundred feet below the plateau level where the "elect of God" lived. A longer view southward was blocked by the protruding mountain slopes which dropped precipitously into the sea without benefit of either plain or beach. In the watchtower the devotee might well have gone from sight to vision, imagining the great future day in the wilderness when the Messiah—priest or king—would appear. Little did he realize that the Messiah was to be or already had been baptized of John in the Jordan to the north of this place.

The daily schedule of the Essenes at Qumran was carefully developed in form and deeply religious in spirit. Before the light of day, complete silence was observed over the whole lonely area except for the droning sound of those who were charged with reading the Torah (Law of Moses) constantly. This practice arose as a result of a literal interpretation of the Scriptural injunction to meditate on the Law day and night. Except for that monotonous sound, all was silent until the first rays of the sun began to appear on the eastern horizon. Gathering from their tents and booths in the assembly room, in the court, or perhaps in other places, the worshipers turned eastward, facing the sun, and in this position with hands outstretched intoned morning prayer. Afterwards, each went to his appointed task, whether menial or responsible. Dressed in white robes, some tilled the soil of the Ain Feshka plain, others made pottery and prepared food, while still others made additions and repairs to the buildings. At approximately 11 A.M., the community gathered for the daily ritual of the holy bath. Each man washed himself in enough cold water for immersion of the entire body, as prescribed in the *Damascus Document*. That manuscript, which was discovered in a *genizah* (a storage place for worn-out Scripture scrolls until proper burial could be carried out) at Cairo by Schechter in 1896 and was published in 1910, gives specific instructions concerning the necessary amount and condition of water for a proper bath.

> Concerning purification with water: Let not a man wash in water that is filthy or not enough for covering a man. Let him not purify in it any vessel. And any pool in a rock in which there is not enough covering, which an unclean person has touched, its water is unclean like the water of a vessel.[2]

When purified by the bath, the community gathered for a sacred meal in the refectory with the overseer blessing bread and wine before he gave it to those who were full-fledged members. After the meal, a prayer of thanks was offered. Since the sect was patiently awaiting the coming of God's Kingdom, its sacred meal represented a foretaste of the feast in that Kingdom, much as the victorious repast is described in the book of Revelation. After the meal, members returned to their work until evening, when another meal was served. Evening prayer was said as the sun passed from sight. These prayers were possibly said with the suppliant facing west. With the advent of darkness, the community dispersed to individual living quarters leaving only a skeletal force at the center where the overseer or bishop had his quarters. Darkness again brought on the silent vigil which continued until the sun appeared next morning. A song of a pious member indicates that community life was organized around the movement of the sun.

> I will praise thy name among those who fear thee,
> with songs of thanksgiving and prayer,
> lying prostrate and making supplication
> continually from period to period;

with the coming in of light from its dwelling,
in the circuits of day in its fixed order,
according to the decrees of the great luminary,
at the turn of evening and the outgoing of light,
at the beginning of the dominion of darkness,
at the appointed time of night in its circuit,
at the turn of morning, and the period of its ingathering
to its dwelling before the light,
at the outgoing of night and the coming in of day . . .[3]

With a schedule set to the movement of the sun, work and worship, meditation and prayer were ordered at Qumran. From year to year the well-established routine of life continued with little if any variation.

Simply to reproduce a schedule does not, however, recover or revive the life of a religious movement. Most of the inhabitants seem to have been male, and their most serious occupation apparently was their study of the Law. Each group of ten technically constituted a congregation having its own priest. One out of every such "sub-congregation" busied himself at study or reading of the Scriptures twenty-four hours a day to make sure that there was never a time at Qumran when the Law of God was not being read aloud and meditated on silently. From the *Manual of Discipline* we read:

And from the place where the ten are there shall never be absent a man who searches the law day and night, by turns, one after another. And the masters shall keep watch together a third of all the nights of the year, reading the book and searching for justice, and worshiping together.[4]

By using three shifts or more, Joshua's exhortation to the

Hebrew people that "This book of the law shall not depart out of thy mouth, but thou shalt meditate thereon day and night," [5] as well as the Psalmist's description of the happy man as one "who doth meditate on his law day and night," [6] were fulfilled seriously and literally. Moreover, study led to the production of commentaries on various books of Scripture, such as the commentaries on Habakkuk, Micah, and Nahum, while the joy of personal faith was expressed in the composition of new psalms. Even though the quality of this poetry is not up to the standard of Biblical Psalms, it represents, none the less, a splendid spiritual expression of profound faith. In the "writing room," however, the most important job was the scribal task of copying Holy Scripture. Whether for this purpose all Qumran's citizens learned to write cannot be known. So far scholars working on the literature of Qumran have identified some four hundred different individual scribes who worked on the documents. Favorite books, to judge from the number of copies discovered, were Deuteronomy and Isaiah, the first because it is basically law, whose interpretation was the divine calling of the community; the second because it provided the general prophetic basis on which the Qumran community was established. Apparently law and prophecy were on an equal footing among the sectarians and each was highly respected as the word of God. Whether some kind of unofficial canon existed is debatable, but the Scriptures were prized highly enough to be the object of continuous copying.

The liturgy of Qumran had no place for sacrifice since the only proper locale for making sacrifice was Jerusalem's Temple. Although the devout of the desert made the sacrifice of their lips in prayer at sunrise, at midday, and at sunset, sacrifices were possibly dispatched to the Temple on a

regular schedule. The Essenes expected to control the Temple
when the Messiah came. However, even in this aspect of
religious life most members studiously avoided direct contact with the corrupt outside world.

Organization at the highest level consisted of a Community Council of twelve laymen and three priests, with a
bishop serving as the chief official in the society. In addition to the bishop, there was an Inspector or Censor who
had charge of instruction and indoctrination along with other
duties. Four distinct classes were recognized in the sect as
it existed elsewhere, and probably the same social stratification was maintained at Qumran. In order of importance,
these strata were Priests, Levites, Children of Israel, and
proselytes. The Children of Israel and the Qumran citizenship were, of course, identical. Whether the proselyte ever
attained full status in the society is doubtful. Moreover,
within the community there was a distinct sense of rank,
based on seniority, with each expected not only to know his
place but to stay in it. Meetings of the congregation were
frequent and evidently were quasi-democratic in spirit, with
rules of order far more stringent than any that Robert has
since devised. A rather stern decorum and discipline was
maintained at all times in the community. A few crimes and
their punishments in terms of banishment will suffice as
illustration:

Bearing a grudge against a fellow	6 months
Taking vengeance against a fellow	6 months
Uttering a foolish word	3 months
Interruption when another is talking	10 days
Sleeping during congregation meeting	30 days
Walking out on congregation meeting three times	10 days

Walking out on congregation meeting after the masters object	30 days
Walking naked before community	6 months
Spitting at the congregation meeting	30 days
Revealing nakedness	30 days
Laughing foolishly	30 days
Slandering a brother	1 year
Slandering community	permanent
Traitor to the truth	2 years [7]

Being banished from community life for ten days in the desert was a heavy punishment to bear, since this meant a reduction in rations. In the more serious offenses, food was probably denied to the offender. Because he had taken a vow to accept nothing from the hands of those outside the fold, such a reprobate could only hope to live on the land, a poor prospect at best. The discipline was severe and was usually very effective.

Many Essene enclaves, if not all, practiced celibacy, making their continued existence dependent upon the entrance of new members into the brotherhood from the outside. It is undeniable that there were some married Essenes but most were not married, which means that the colony was not biologically self-perpetuating. The process by which one became a member of the sect was rather involved. First, the applicant appeared before the Inspector of the community; and, when found acceptable, he entered a period of probation, the length of which is not certain. At the end of that first period, he was examined concerning his progress which, when satisfactory, made him a novitiate for one year. After one year in the community, following a trial, he went into the last year of initiation. Having been examined by the Inspector for a second time before the members and having taken "tremendous oaths," the novitiate became a junior member. His final entrance required the vote of the entire community, which in effect made him a part of the True Israel. At the end of the first year within the brotherhood, he was permitted to take part in the sacred baths with other full-fledged members. The bath thus served as a preliminary rite of initiation while continuing to be a daily ritual. The Essene felt that to have effect, the ritual bath—like repentance for the Christian or Jew—needed to be repeated each day. At the end of the final year of preparation, the fledgling or novitiate was allowed to partake of the sacred meal with others, according to his rank. He was under obligation always to protect the secrets of the community—being ready to die rather than divulge them; to love the other members of the sect; and to show respect at all times for his superiors. The initiatory ceremony followed this order:

Promise
    New member promises to be faithful to death.
    Recounting of God's deliverances told by priests and
        Levites.
    The initiate says Amen.
Confession
    God is righteous say the priests.
    Israel is iniquitous says the Levite.
    The initiate confesses his sin.
Benediction
    Priests bless all men who serve God.
Curses
    Against the sons of perversion.
    The initiate says Amen.

When a man joined the Qumran group and was accepted into full membership, he was required to sell all property, which was despised by the community as being evil, and to contribute the income to the commonwealth of the group. All property was handled by a single steward. No exchange of property or financial transaction of any kind was permitted within the brotherhood itself since such activity would *per se* violate the idea of community as it was understood among them. The Essenes rejoiced in their poverty, considering material possessions to be a deterrent to individual spiritual development. Even their clothing, simple as it was, was held in common and was worn to shreds before disposal. Lying concerning wealth by an initiate was a most heinous offense. Any individual joining the Qumran sect gave up all ties with the world outside the confines of this desert retreat.

Living in the desert during those turbulent times prior to and early in the Christian era only partially isolated the sect from the cruel and corrupt world. Alexander Jannaeus persecuted these Essenes with an unbelievable severity early in the first century, probably killing many of this particular group. It is possible that the colony hoped for better things with the appearance of the Romans in 63 B.C., but by the time the *Commentary on Habakkuk* was written, the Romans had become the oppressors *par excellence*. Herod the Great, ruling at the sufferance of Rome, forced the Essenes out of their desert home when he began to construct a palace at Jericho, probably not wishing to have so strict a sect as eyewitnesses to his own questionable private behavior. Not until A.D. 6 or thereabout did the group return to live again at Qumran. Meanwhile, the brotherhood probably went back to Damascus, becoming a part of an Essene community there for the interim. From A.D. 6 to 68, the colony flourished without serious interruption or interference.

In this general period there was born in Bethlehem a baby

named Jesus, who at the age of manhood became a well-known itinerant rabbi. His kinsman, John the Baptist, began a ministry in the wilderness of Judaea (Matthew 3:1) and doubtless came in contact with the Essene brotherhood. It was to this region that Jesus went for His temptation experience (Matthew 4:1-11) and here Paul withdrew for his spiritual retreat (Galatians 1:17). The disciples of John who later followed Jesus were also well acquainted with the desert area in which Qumran was located. (John 1:28-51.) That there was contact between the Master, as well as early leaders of the Church, and the Qumran community cannot be doubted. Side by side the Church and the Qumran community developed, with inevitable influence one upon the other, especially after A.D. 68 when Essenes in considerable numbers presumably began to unite with the Church. Even before that, however, these contemporary organizations drawing from the Old Testament traditions and customs showed marked similarities.

The Qumran community was a representative group of the third great Jewish religious party of New Testament times. Pharisees and Sadducees are well known through frequent references in contemporary and subsequent records. Now the Essenes have emerged from the shadows and are seen in the clear light of day. That they were contemporaries of Jesus and the early Church is a fact which cannot be forgotten; in fact, it is for this reason alone that this book is being published. Widespread interest in the scrolls has arisen because of the contact with Christianity in its earliest and most formative period.

Before proceeding to discuss affinities between the two movements, we shall mention only briefly a few distinctive features of the Essene faith as gleaned from the documents of the Dead Sea region. First, there was a very strict adherence to the Law of Moses as the means by which one became a true Israelite. Literal interpretation was characteristic of the community. Sabbath law serves as the best illustration. The Law as interpreted by the Essenes forbade trifling talk, borrowing or lending, and talking about tomorrow's work. According to their rule, members were allowed to eat only what was prepared, to drink only what was in camp. The distance one might travel was also limited. Essenes were told not to take up a suckling child to go in or out, not to help the ox in the ditch, and not to give aid to an animal bearing young on the Sabbath. These and many other proscriptions were recorded. The single most amazing Sabbath proscription is this one from the *Damascus Document:*

> And if any person falls into a place of water, or into a place, let not a man come up by a ladder or rope or instrument.[8]

Strict adherence to the Law was, of course, based on a more fundamental aspect of theology, namely, the sovereignty of God. Even a cursory reading of the literature reveals a complete dependence upon God, who is recognized as the creator of all things and with whom all events originate. Man is only the agent through whom God works! Divine election was a corollary to this scheme with full membership in the community equivalent to approval by God and security in His Kingdom.

Together with this doctrine of God's sovereign power and election of a Righteous Remnant, there arose also a doctrine of two spirits which God created at the beginning, namely a spirit of truth and a spirit of error—a spirit of light and a spirit of darkness—a spirit of righteousness and a spirit of perversion. These two spirits struggled against each other at every level of life from the individual soul to the small group and finally to the international stage. Struggle was the texture of life and history. Mankind was divided into two distinct groups: the sons of Darkness and the sons of Light. Choice had nothing to do with what a man was. At the end of history and only then would the struggle be resolved. In the final victory of God, darkness would be banished, together with all who served in its ranks.

In preparation for the last great battle of history, the Essenes kept alive a liturgy for Holy War, even though they themselves were pacifists. Undoubtedly the military formations and terminology of the War Scroll were carry-overs from the Maccabean Revolt. Like modern Jehovah's Witnesses, who are conscientious objectors, there was a readiness to fight valiantly in the final battle of history (that is, Armageddon). Whether this colony of Essenes fought in the Jewish revolt of A.D. 67-70 because they believed the rebellion was the battle of Armageddon cannot be determined. It is quite probable that they did. In any case, they foresaw a final battle in which the righteous would fight and God would prevail. In that hope they possibly threw themselves against the Roman legions in A.D. 67-68, but to no avail.

The Essenes believed that they were living in the final age and that very soon the era of God's triumphant Kingdom was to begin. They expected two Messiahs of Israel and Aaron, a king and priest, but in addition they anticipated the coming of a prophet before the advent of the priestly and kingly Messiahs. Exactly when and how these Messiahs would appear is not clear. Actually it was this expectation that kept alive the priesthood in the community even though no sacrifices were made locally. At the inception of the new age, Temple sacrifices would begin anew and priests would be once more a necessity. Meanwhile the priest presided over the Holy Meal in place of the Messiah who was yet to appear.

Qumran lived in the serene confidence of God's sovereign care and looked forward with hope to the Messianic Age which was about to dawn. Meanwhile, small as the group was, with their number reduced by death, the members thought themselves to be the only True Israel, the People of the Covenant. When the Messiahs came, they would confirm their membership in the community and establish their rule with power. Like their beloved founder, the Messiahs would be Teachers of Righteousness. Even though the great age was about to dawn, history so long as it continued was to be understood as a struggle which God had ordained. The problem of God's having been the author of evil did not seem to disturb the desert dwellers. While the struggle continued, the elect of God only waited to see its victorious consummation. In the meantime, the Righteous Remnant must preserve itself.

So the desert has begun to reveal its well-kept secret and has started to give to the reader a new insight into the past. The origins of the Qumran sect and the reason for its development are almost impossible to trace with complete accuracy, but such is not the case with its passage from the historical scene. A Jewish revolt against Rome began in A.D. 67 and continued for three years, ending in the utter decimation of Jerusalem and her Temple. With systematic Roman thoroughness, Vespasian and his Tenth Legion began the Palestine campaign by destroying all inhabited places around the Jerusalem-Jericho area. One such place was Qumran.

Prior to the inevitable destruction of their center and its

environs by Rome, the members of the community carefully packed many of their most precious scrolls in large pottery jars, covering the tops with linen and sealing them with some sort of pitch. Time probably did not allow for any such care for all documents, so some were placed unpacked in a man-made underground room near the center (i.e., Cave IV). Some of the scrolls were carried to the caves where members lived from time to time, and they were left there for safekeeping until an opportunity to return might present itself. No such time ever came. Hence the scrolls remained in the caves and other places of hiding until most recent times.

The Romans demolished the community center, tearing down its tower and walls, leaving the proud building a shambles and wrecking the water system which was so much a part of life in the desert. Apparently uninterested in any possible loot which these poverty-stricken desert dwellers might have possessed, the Romans, having wrecked the center, moved on to Jerusalem, whose promised treasures were more enticing. After A.D. 68 Qumran was never again an organized functioning community, but the spot served for some years as a Roman fort. The membership either fled or was massacred.

Yet Qumran and its Essene inhabitants continued to live on in the influence which they had already exerted on the early leaders of the newly formed Christian Church. After A.D. 68, many Essenes became Christians and helped to shape several facets of the early Church's faith and life. It is to this important contribution of the community at Qumran that we shall turn our attention in the remainder of the book. But before that, a cursory survey of the discoveries must be given.

2. *Treasure Trove*

IN WRITING FOR the lay reader, one is always tempted to pass over a repetitive cataloguing of manuscripts and other written source material. Accounts of the discovery of Cave I near Khirbet Qumran are already so numerous that to repeat the story would be superfluous. In fact, the original account has changed many times by interpretations and accretions according to the point of view of the storyteller, making an objective account hard to recapture. None the less, we cannot avoid a brief survey of what has been discovered, identified, and catalogued to this time. Our list is not complete, but it will at least indicate the extensiveness of these finds and their present state of preservation.

To date, at least eleven caves have produced manuscripts of some sort, most of them extremely fragmentary. The announcement of the Cave XI discovery was made in 1956 but the contents are not available for study. Of the four most recently discovered caves, before Cave XI, it can only be said that the condition of the unearthed pieces is bad and their quantity is exceedingly small. Some caves have collapsed, burying the bits and tatters under several feet of dirt, and leaving them, after 1900 years, in an advanced state of decay. Most recently, Arabs have appeared with an authentic copy of Leviticus, the purchase of which is being negotiated while the manuscript itself is kept in a safe place. This is the first complete scroll which has appeared since the original discovery some nine years ago. Reports of the discovery of the entire Pentateuch are erroneous, having little or no foundation in fact. However, it is true that a copper scroll preserved in two parts was unearthed some time ago and is presently housed in the museum at Amman, Jordan. On it are lists of alleged places where the "treasures of the Hebrew people" were hidden, hence its discovery caused a brief flurry of excitement in the popular press. What the nature of these treasures was and whether they ever existed except in the minds of the Qumran community is debatable.

The First Scrolls

Isaiah. A complete scroll of Isaiah, with the full sixty-six chapters in a good state of preservation, was found in Cave I together with other manuscripts listed below. This copy was made toward the end of the second century B.C. and is the oldest complete manuscript of Isaiah in existence. Generally speaking, it follows the text reflected in the major English translations of our Bible.

Isaiah. A second and later manuscript of Isaiah was brought to Hebrew University, where it was published. It is neither so complete nor so well preserved as the first one of the same prophet. Totally lacking from this Isaiah manuscript, which was published by the late Professor E. L. Sukenik of Hebrew University, are chapters 1-9, 11, 12, 14, 15, 17, 18, 21, 24, 25, 27, 31-34, 36, and 42.

Manual of Discipline. Originally this scroll was called *The Sectarian Document* by Millar Burrows and others, but now these rules of faith and order for the community are identified as *The Manual of Discipline*. Additional parts of other copies of this same work have since been discovered in various caves. The content of this scroll bears ideological resemblances to the *Damascus Document,* discovered at Cairo in 1896 and published in 1910 by Solomon Schechter.

Thanksgiving Psalms.   Probably these songs represent the latest manuscript in the original cache. Written in good Hebrew style, the psalms reflect at once the theology and devotional life of the individual Essene.

Habakkuk Commentary.   Devout students of the Bible have always interpreted the ancient word in contemporary context. Taking section by section, Essene scholars applied the ancient prophecy of Habakkuk to their own day, seeing the fulfillment of prophecy in the events of their lifetime. Probably the commentary comes from the last half of the first century B.C.

The War of the Sons of Light with the Sons of Darkness. This scroll, which contains rules for Holy War, is the most peculiar in content of all those discovered. A sort of liturgy is combined with the record of outmoded military formations used during the Maccabean Revolt and the promise of victory in the final battle for God. Apparently a non-violent people were kept "at ready" in case they should be momentarily called upon to fight in the final battle of history.

The Genesis Commentary.   For several years this scroll, in such a bad state of preservation, could not be unrolled or read. On the basis of the examination of a corner which had been "accidentally" broken off it was identified some years ago as the book of Lamech, whose name appeared in the separate fragment. For these eight years and more, scholars have referred to the Lamech Scroll; however, with the recent unrolling of it, no Lamech apocalypse appeared; it turned out to be a version of and commentary on Genesis. In it the text is interspersed with otherwise unknown apoc-

ryphal details from the lives of the Patriarchs. Work on
the scroll has been undertaken by two Israeli scholars, Nahmen Avigad and Yigael Yadin, and their preliminary find-
ings have been published in Jerusalem under the title, *A
Genesis Apocryphon.* An interesting description of Sarah's
beauty is given in connection with Genesis 12; a fascinating
portrayal of the land is appended to chapter 13; a vivid
cataloguing of names and places is given in connection with
the war of chapter 14. Other fascinating, late, apocryphal
material about the Patriarchal Age is even now forthcoming
(e.g. Noah, Lamech, *et al*). Details can be had through
reading the work of Avigad and Yadin.

Later Discoveries

These seven manuscripts were the original scrolls from
Cave I, but since that chance discovery other fragments have
been brought from the same cave. Among Biblical pieces
found are parts of Genesis, Exodus, Leviticus, Deuteronomy, Judges, Samuel, Isaiah, Ezekiel, and Psalms. In addition, commentaries on Micah, Proverbs, and Psalms have
been found. Apochryphal works include the Book of Jubilees, the Book of Noah, Apocalypse of Lamech, Testament
of Levi, Sayings of Moses, Book of Mysteries, and so forth.
Hymns together with legal and liturgical texts have also been
identified from the same cave.

Most productive among the caves was Cave IV, where
literally tens of thousands of fragments have been discovered. Already three hundred and thirty manuscripts have
been identified, of which ninety are Biblical. Even so, except
for Esther, at least some portion of every book in the Hebrew
canon has been uncovered.

Since a complete cataloguing of the scrolls is not necessary for our purposes, one other find is mentioned more for its curiosity value than for its direct relationship to our subject, that is, the previously referred to Copper Scroll. This scroll has been cut in strips and has been read, but its contents are of little importance to this study. Indeed it may represent the imaginative work of one Essene, not the whole community.

Needless to say, these manuscripts throw tremendous light on Old Testament studies and on the inter-Testament period, but those facets of the discoveries do not come within the scope of this volume. We now move into those areas where Qumran seems to have vitally touched and influenced Christianity.

3.

John the Baptist and the Essenes

A MAN NAMED John appeared in the wilderness of Judaea just prior to the public ministry of Jesus. In fact, this same prophetic figure is linked with Jesus at the time of his birth according to the Lukan Gospel account, where he is said to be the son of the priest Zacharias and his wife, Elisabeth, when both were well beyond the usual child-producing age. John was a child of great wonder whose life was made possible by direct, divine intervention. His father, having been struck speechless for lack of faith when the annunciation was made, wrote the name "John" on a piece of paper; and the child was ever after known by that name though there was no near kinsman or ancestor bearing such a name. During Elisabeth's pregnancy she was visited by her cousin, Mary, and they rejoiced together over prospective motherhood. After the lovely Magnificat, and the Benedictus of Zacharias, we are tersely told this about the boy:

> "And the child grew, and waxed strong in spirit, and was in the deserts till the day of his showing unto Israel." [1]

Of course, one must allow for some elaboration of the story, but even so the general tradition concerning John can be accepted as accurate.

Obviously, John was from a local priestly line which did not serve at the Temple in Jerusalem. For some reason, he withdrew into the wilderness of the Jordan and there, according to tradition, grew to manhood. Until recently, one could say with some confidence that life in the desert could not be sustained over long periods of time. Hence, this tradition was not to be taken seriously. Now we know of one community which did subsist rather well in the arid region generally known as the wilderness of Judaea. Exactly what was John's relationship to this sect which dwelt on the Qumran plateau?

William Brownlee of Duke University makes a strong case for John's having been reared by the Essenes, but it is more likely that he was attached to some other enclave nearby. Certainly there is no objective evidence that he ever entered the Essene center as a full-fledged member. Neither is there sufficient proof to conclude that he grew up with the desert group. Precedent for parents' allowing a child to go to a shrine and grow up there is found in the story of Samuel (I Samuel 1-3), whose mother, Hannah, sent him to Shiloh to live under the tutelage of Eli. Still, this does not necessarily mean that John followed the Samuel tradition. Getting a child away from the evil influences of the city is not a new desire among parents; but there were many places in the desert, other than Qumran, where he might have been sent. It is possible that his parents sent him to some secluded place, or that upon reaching adulthood he went there of his own volition. In any case, John grew up somewhere in the wilderness and was in some measure acquainted with the Essene enclave at Qumran. Exactly what his relationship to the Qumran religious society was cannot be fully determined on the basis of present material in hand. However, there is no doubt that John's contact with Essenism was direct and probably personal.

It is improbable that John was an Essene since he did not withdraw as completely as they did, nor did he despair of calling the outside world to God. Moreover, the baptism of John was apparently unrepeatable, being more sacramental in character than the baths of Qumran and having no connection with priestly functions and traditions.

According to the Gospel accounts, John was only about thirty or in his early thirties when he began his ministry. His life had undoubtedly known the play of Essene influence, which movement he certainly must have known from the outside. John met emissaries from the community who had come to the caravan town of Bethany beyond the Jordan (Bethabara) and to another trading post at Aenon for supplies. In fact, this might well prove to be the only direct contact which he ever had with the settlement of Qumran. He began to preach about repentance and baptism, which he had heard from several sources including the Old Testament, the Pharisees, and the Essenes; but there was a distinctive note of urgency in his own peculiar message. Not being a member of the brotherhood, he was not fully versed in the esoteric aspect of Essenic doctrine but at least was able to proclaim to the world some of the more obvious features which were shared by Qumran. When he began to preach a militant, prophetic doctrine to the world, he started at the same localities where he had met Essenes, some of whom might well have been among the large congregations which assembled there. Of course, a final resolution of this problem cannot be had with incomplete records of both John and the Qumran sect, but the above suggestions seem to fit present evidence.

John was a man dressed in animal skins who lived on locusts and wild honey. (Matthew 3:4.) In fact, his loincloth was very similar to that which was uniform among the Essenes. Apparently he shared the Essenic disdain for the world, having been so long a recluse that all people were to him a "generation of vipers." (Luke 3:7, K.J.V.) To them he spoke, however, not only a word of judgment but also a message of hope.

The preaching of John may be clearly catalogued, as follows:

CONCERNING THE MESSIAH

1. After me there comes one who is mightier than I, the thong of whose sandal I am unworthy to stoop down and loosen.
2. I baptize you with water, but he will baptize you with the Holy Spirit . . .
3. His fan is in his hand and he will cleanse his threshing floor and gather his grain together in the granary, but the chaff he will burn with unquenchable fire. . . .

PROCLAMATION

4. Brood of vipers, who has showed you that you will escape the coming wrath?
5. Produce fruits worthy of repentance, and do not think to say, "We have Abraham for our father," for I tell you God can raise up children to Abraham from these stones.
6. Already the axe lies at the root of the trees. Every tree, therefore, that does not bring forth good fruit will be cut down and thrown into the fire.

IN ANSWER TO QUESTIONS

7. The crowds asked him saying, "What are we to do?" But he answered saying to them, "Whoever has two shirts, let him share with him who has none, and whoever has food, let him do likewise."

8. The tax-collectors came to be baptized and said to him, "What are we to do?" But he said to them, "Exact no more than the established tax rate allows."

9. Even the soldiers asked him saying, "And what are we to do?" And he said to them, "Do not apply violence for personal gain; do not lay false charges; and be satisfied with your wages." [2]

This is essentially what John preached. His relationship to Jesus and the connection between the early Church and the movement started by John are of importance to this discussion only in that there is such a close connection between John's group and the Christian community that what affects one influences both.

According to tradition, John baptized Jesus in the Jordan (Matthew 3:13-17) and continued to baptize many at Aenon, where much water was (John 3:23-24). The baptism of John had its origin with proselyte baptism in general and had some connection with Qumran lustration in particular. Every convert to Judaism from the Gentile world was required to be immersed, after which he submitted to circumcision followed by the making of a sacrifice. Under certain circumstances, however, the convert was not required either to be circumcised or to make a sacrifice. The ceremony of immersion presided over by proper religious authority, therefore, became *per se* the essential rite of initiation into Judaism.

John called upon men to repent before baptism, but to this change of heart and ceremony of cleansing he called not only non-Jews but Jews as well. He was calling on the people thus to claim their true heritage in Israel. The Jew, having been corrupted by the world, had become a spiritual

Gentile and needed to be washed. It would seem, therefore, that John was seeking to call out a New Israel from society in general through repentance and baptism.

In Qumran, the daily bath was routine, but only those who had passed the novitiate state were allowed to participate. Since the baths were private, it is probable that John even if he visited Qumran did not know the significance of daily lustration. However, meeting as he did with Essenes, he had surely heard about the initial immersion by which one became a part of the community. He followed this aspect which he knew but not the repetitive bath-practice of the Essenes. Baptism as practiced by John was never self-administered as it surely was at Qumran. John gave to baptism his own new interpretation.

John the Baptist can be said to have taken the idea of baptism from the Qumran community although he was never a member of the group. His disdain for the world is typically Essene but not uniquely so. The call to repentance is little more than an echo from the prophets in whose line John must be placed, but it is possibly an echo which came via the Essenes and other sectarian groups of the desert. The fact that John was himself conscious of being in the great tradition of the prophets has not been altered by recent discoveries.

John's development diverged from that at Qumran. Since there is no evidence of a violent break or any polemic against the Essenes, the above explanation seems to fit. The divergences between John and Qumran resulted from the fact that the Baptist and Essene movements are parallel, growing out of the same general historical, psychological, and ideological background. Having contact with the world at Aenon and Bethany, he spoke an oracle of judgment and gave a call to repentance where men were. In doing this, he was in the best tradition of the great prophets.

The differences between John and the community at Qumran increased with the passage of time. Such a development would be expected, for John is in many ways a dynamic and original figure who sought to prepare in the desert a highway for the Messiah by calling all men to repentance. His vision of the Kingdom was greater than that held by the Essenes. Deeds of righteousness were not to him stereotyped as at Qumran but consisted rather of practical honesty and justice.

Finally, John was the forerunner of the Messiah and, therefore, succeeded in preparing the way in the desert for Christ's coming. He baptized the founder of the Christian movement and subordinated his ministry to that of Jesus. Some of John's disciples became the disciples of Jesus, exerting an undeterminable influence in the Christian community from the outset. Influences which played on the Baptizer's movement ultimately, though indirectly, also had a bearing on the Church. This is especially true with respect to the sacrament of baptism.

4.   *Sacraments and Worship*

Baptism

AMONG EARLY CHRISTIANS there was recognized
some distinct difference between the baptism of John and
that administered by the Church. Support for this conclusion comes when Paul at Ephesus (Acts 19:1-7) discovered a group of John's followers who had not yet been
baptized with the Holy Spirit but had received only the
preliminary immersion of the Baptist movement. Actually,
early believers in Christ did not stress this initiatory act
as much as did the Baptist group, a fact reflected in Paul's
apparent depreciation of the primacy of baptism.

> "Christ sent me not to baptize, but to preach the gospel:
> not in wisdom of words, lest the cross of Christ should
> be made void." (I Corinthians 1:17.)

Even so, baptism became the initiatory rite of the ancient
Church in a stricter sense than it was at Qumran, since
in the Church all converts submitted to it as a mark of their
inclusion. Prior to acceptance into the Church, inquiry was
made and frequently a period of probation was prescribed.
Baptism for the Church, as for John the Baptist, was an
initiatory and unrepeatable act which made it different
from the practice at Qumran where a daily symbolic bath
or self-administered baptism was on the schedule.
That the baths at the community center influenced atti-

tudes and events within the Christian community cannot
be doubted in the light of a well-known incident between
Jesus and His disciples recorded by the writer of the Fourth
Gospel. In the account, during the Passover meal Jesus took
a basin, water, and a towel and began to wash His disciples'
feet. (John 13:1-11.) This account was included in the
Gospel to illustrate and to recommend humility to the Christian Church by holding up to the faithful the example of
their Master. However, when Jesus came to Peter in the
process of going from disciple to disciple, this conversa-
tional exchange occurred between the two:

Peter: "Lord, dost thou wash my feet?"
Jesus: "What I do thou knowest not now; but thou
        shalt understand hereafter."
Peter: "Thou shalt never wash my feet."
Jesus: "If I wash thee not, thou hast no part with me."
Peter: "Lord, not my feet only, but also my hands and
        my head."
Jesus: "He that is bathed needeth not save to wash his
        feet, but is clean every whit: and ye are clean,
        but not all." [1]

Apparently, Simon Peter at first misunderstood the intent
of Jesus. He saw this gesture only as a simple act of humility,
as indeed it was, so he was reluctant to allow his Lord thus
to be humiliated. Jesus answered this reluctance with a
cryptic saying from which Peter drew the conclusion that
this was in fact an institution of some kind of ritual bath.
Immediately the apostle suggested that he be washed all
over, but Jesus rejected complete bathing or constant bathing as He stressed the fact that believers are already clean.
This incident shows that the Church was not only conscious
of Essenic practice but was in some measure influenced di-

rectly by it. Peter's desire undoubtedly arose because he had heard about this practice among the Essenes. According to John's account, the suggestion was clearly rejected by Jesus.

The form of Christian baptism was, in all probability, borrowed from the practice of baptizing converts to Judaism. Variations of this practice are represented both in the John the Baptist movement and in the Essene community. Dependable tradition is insistent that Jesus Himself was baptized by John. The sacrament of baptism, so far as form goes, paralleled the Essene practice, but as used in the Church it became quite different from the rite at Qumran. Among the Essenes, immersion was repeated daily. But this was not possible in the Church, where Christians undergoing baptism experienced a permanent inner cleansing and re-creation by the Holy Spirit. Moreover, for the Essenes this was not really the initiatory ceremony but occurred one year prior to the convert's entrance into the brotherhood; only after a second year of probation did the initiate partake of the Holy Meal. The Holy Meal, not baptism, was *de facto* the initiatory act at Qumran. On the other hand, baptism was initiatory for the Church because it was an outward symbol of an inward change. Furthermore, the Church administered this sacrament in the name of the Trinity, which was not part of Essene dogma.

Baptism's meaning as it developed in the early Church was quite different from the Qumran concept of the ritual bath. The burial-resurrection motif is clearly described by Paul in Romans 6:3-7.

"Are ye ignorant that all we who were baptized into Christ Jesus were baptized into his death? We were buried therefore with him through baptism into death:

that like as Christ was raised from the dead through the glory of the Father, so we also might walk in newness of life. For if we have become united with him in the likeness of his death, we shall be also in the likeness of his resurrection; knowing this, that our old man was crucified with him, that the body of sin might be done away, that so we should no longer be in bondage to sin; for he that hath died is justified from sin."

The Church extended the symbolism from a washing away of uncleanness, which facet of the baptismal rite it shared with the Essenes, to a burial ceremony. As the body was immersed, the old man died and a new man came to life; thus every Christian entered into and shared the death-resurrection experience of his Master through baptism.

The Church is indebted to Qumran for the form, not the content, of baptism. To the Christian, baptism of a sincere believer is concurrent with God's gift of His Spirit and new life in Christ. The Essenes had no such doctrine; only the rite was theirs!

The Lord's Supper

The Essenic communion meal before noon was the high point of the daily schedule in the brotherhood of Qumran. Participation in this sacred repast was closely guarded, and admission to it was granted only after the most thorough-going period of preparation and probation. The similarity between this Holy Meal and the Lord's Supper or Eucharist has been noted since life in the Qumran community was first brought to light. Of special interest was the fragment which actually described the procedure for the Holy Meal itself. As translated by Dr. Frank M. Cross in *Journal of Biblical Literature*, it reads:

This is the (order of the) session of the "Men of the Name Who Are Invited to the Feast" for the counsel of the Community (when God sends the Messiah to be with them):

The Priest shall enter at the head of all the congregation of Israel and all the fathers of the Aaronids . . . and they shall sit before him. . . .

Next the Messiah of Israel shall enter; and the heads of the thousands of Israel . . . and all the heads of the fathers of the congregation together with the scholars . . . shall sit before him.

They shall sit (arranged) before the (two) of them, each by rank.

[When they solemnly meet at the table of communion, or to drink the wine, the whole communion table is arranged and the wine is mixed for drinking, one shall not stretch out his hand on the first portion of bread or of wine before the Messiah-Priest; for he shall bless the first portion of the bread and wine and stretch out his hand on the bread first of all. Afterwards the Messiah of Israel shall stretch forth his hands on the bread and after giving his blessing, all the congregation of the community shall partake each according to his rank.]

And they shall follow this prescription whenever the meal is arranged, when as many as ten meet together.[2]

What is described in this manuscript is not a memorial meal, as the Lord's Supper later became for the Church, but primarily and simply a meal of anticipation. Christians are familiar with the concept of a great feast of God's Kingdom at its final consummation. (Revelation 19:9.) Christ Himself anticipated some such celebration, which was normative to Judaism generally, when He ate the last supper with His

disciples. Luke represents the thought of Jesus when He sat
with His disciples:

> "With desire I have desired to eat this passover with
> you before I suffer: for I say unto you, I shall not eat
> it, until it be fulfilled in the kingdom of God. . . . I
> shall not drink from henceforth of the fruit of the vine,
> until the kingdom of God shall come." (Luke 22:15-18.)

The conclusion is safe, therefore, that the role of Messiah
was taken by Jesus, who actually was the Messiah, and that
a feast of anticipation became also a memorial meal. The
great meal of consummation to which Christian and Essene
looked forward is described in Revelation 19:9 as the marriage feast of the Lamb.

Early development of the Lord's Supper indicates that
it became more or less a church supper, emphasizing *koin-
onia* (fellowship, oneness) within the Christian community,
even as it did in Qumran. However, since control was apparently not nearly so complete in the Church, soon the
affair became in some cases little more than a gala social
event. This condition existed in Corinth, causing Paul to
write a strong indictment of those who had allowed the
sacred meal to disintegrate so markedly.

> "When therefore ye assemble yourselves together, it
> is not possible to eat the Lord's supper: for in your
> eating each one taketh before other his own supper; and
> one is hungry, and another is drunken. What, have ye
> not houses to eat and to drink in? or despise ye the
> church of God, and put them to shame that have not?
> What shall I say to you? shall I praise you? In this I
> praise you not." (I Corinthians 11:20-22.)

In order to understand the Lord's Supper, which has numerous facets, it is necessary to trace its development to the point where Paul separated it from the common meal of the Christian community.

During the lifetime of Jesus, the Master often enjoyed meals with His disciples, thereby developing a custom which His followers naturally cherished long after His ascension. Moreover, in the post-resurrection appearances, the Lord broke bread on the road to Emmaus and ate a meal on the Galilean shore. There can be little question that this fellowship which the disciples had with their Master in life was continued in His memory. To gather in this way not only made them able to recapture happy moments of another day but also allowed the group individually and collectively to apprehend His spiritual presence in their midst.

Moreover, Jesus was Himself crucified during the Passover season, and a definite connection was drawn between His death and the slaying of the paschal lamb usually slain at the beginning of the celebration. According to the record Jesus gathered together His disciples for a last meal in an upper room and there He transformed the elements of bread and wine into memorial symbols, so that henceforth these physical objects were to become the reminder of His sacrifice on the cross. Jesus certainly attached a redemptive import not only to His life but also to His death. However, being Himself man, He may have been unable to discern the time lapse between His imminent death and His triumphant return. In any case, in the Last Supper Jesus instituted a memorial meal; but He celebrated also an anticipatory feast of victory. From earliest times the Church recognized in the sacrament these two elements.

The Christian community, being primarily not an organization but a loosely knit fellowship whose members shared one faith in Jesus Christ and His teachings, was drawn to express its oneness in the Lord in many ways, the most important of which was the *agape* or love feast. Congregations gathered for a love feast, really a festive occasion, not unlike some of the Jewish festivals before it. As part of this dramatic celebration of the community, bread and wine were passed and their meaning explained. As has been indicated above, however, the festival spirit sometimes got out of hand and this church supper became little more than a secular feast. Wisely the Apostle Paul, seeing the abuse among the Corinthians, separated the *agape* feast from the Lord's Supper, and the latter became distinctly sacramental in nature.

Jesus understood the Church in terms of the New Israel, that is, the People of God, and the Lord's Supper as the Passover for the New Community. To some extent He began to identify His followers with the new society of God, substituting the sacrament for the Passover, making of it a dramatic reminder of the redemption wrought in the death-resurrection event. Even as the Passover had been for the Jews a celebration of their redemption from bondage in Egypt, so the Lord's Supper became an equally meaningful portrayal of redemption from the greater bondage to which all men are subject.

The words of institution of this Supper as found in the Gospels and in Paul's writings are records reflecting the nature and practice of the rite in the early Church. Mark's account is based on very early tradition.

> "And as they were eating, he took bread, and when he had blessed, he brake it, and gave to them, and said, Take ye: this is my body. And he took a cup, and when he had given thanks, he gave to them: and they all

> drank of it. And he said unto them, This is my blood
> of the covenant, which is poured out for many. Verily
> I say unto you, I shall no more drink of the fruit of the
> vine, until that day when I drink it new in the kingdom
> of God." (Mark 14:22-25.)

Some minor textual accretions inevitably may have attached to this statement of Jesus, but such must have occurred early in the life of the Church. Nobody can doubt for a moment that this is a memorial meal which henceforth in a sense took the place of sacrifice for the Church. The cup and the loaf were from the outset entwined with the meaning of the Teacher's life and work.

In the Gospel of John, which may well reflect the situation in the early Church, symbolic feeding on Christ is explained in physical terminology. This was done in response to a heretical group or groups who had begun to feel that Jesus in the flesh was an illusion; for flesh as such, according to this view, was inherently evil. The words of Jesus are recorded by John in this way:

> "Verily, verily, I say unto you, Except ye eat the flesh
> of the Son of man and drink his blood, ye have not life
> in yourselves. He that eateth my flesh and drinketh my
> blood hath eternal life; and I will raise him up at the
> last day. For my flesh is meat indeed, and my blood is
> drink indeed. He that eateth my flesh and drinketh my
> blood abideth in me, and I in him." (John 6:53-56.)

Mystical union with Christ thus became for Christians a part of the symbolic meal.

Paul gave these words of institution of the Lord's Supper:

> "For I received of the Lord that which also I delivered

unto you, that the Lord Jesus in the night in which he
was betrayed took bread; and when he had given thanks,
he brake it, and said, This is my body, which is for you:
this do in remembrance of me. In like manner also the
cup, after supper, saying, This cup is the new covenant
in my blood: this do, as often as ye drink it, in remembrance of me. For as often as ye eat this bread, and
drink the cup, ye proclaim the Lord's death till he
come." (I Corinthians 11:23-26.)

The convergence of these sources yields a vivid picture of
the Lord's Supper and its meaning. It was a celebration of
the new community which was the Church, wherein union
with Christ and with each other was dramatically enacted.
Moreover, this meal was both a memorial to the death-
resurrection event, with the symbolic food specifically explained, and at the same time an anticipatory feast of the
Coming Kingdom. In ancient congregations there was in the
meal a memory of the death, but almost more important
was an apprehension of the living presence. The joy of knowing Christ in the sacrament was for the Church simply a
foretaste and promise of reunion with Him.

The history of this sacrament in the Christian Church follows lines which have been traced, but development of the
sacred meal at Qumran was different. Bread and wine were
blessed by a priest of the brotherhood who stood in place
of the expected Messiah, in anticipation of his advent. Keen
expectation was definitely an element in the first-century
atmosphere, which was charged with excitement over the
impending advent of God's Kingdom. In addition to this
aspect of the Holy Meal at Qumran, it was a community
affair expressive of the fellowship which the brotherhood
had with each other. In these two facets there is a marked

similarity between early Christianity and Essenism—in their respective common meals.

Differences, however, far outweigh the similarities. The sacrament of the Lord's Supper was a memorial meal with symbolic elements, memorializing a Messiah who had already come and would come again. Christians connected the Supper with the Lord's death and resurrection, consciously substituting it for the Passover of Judaism. Communion with the Messiah's risen presence was another difference. Suffice it to say that the elements which are similar in the two meals are drawn from the common background of the Hebrew faith. Beyond that, each development in the Lord's Supper made it increasingly different from the Essene meal both in content and practice.

The exact form of the meal as practiced in Qumran influenced the development of the Lord's Supper. Even so, except for a few externals there are no similarities. To equate the two in meaning is the height of folly. That there was parallel development out of a common source is the most that can be concluded from the evidence.

Daily Prayer

The exact schedule of daily prayer at Qumran is not certain, but it seems to have had a direct relation to the course of the sun's rising and setting. Matins and vespers were regular times for worship as they later became in the Christian Church. Perhaps the later emphasis has some tenuous connection with the Essene sect.

Strong tradition supported the Jewish practice of three daily prayers, as is illustrated in the devotion of Daniel (Daniel 6:10) and by the author of Psalm 55:17. The Christian Church very early picked up this practice as a part of its ordinary life. Peter and John are said to have gone up to the Temple at the hour of prayer, being the ninth hour or about 3 p.m., a time which coincides with the second of three daily prayers prescribed in Judaism. Since this petition was raised at the hour of evening sacrifice it would seem possible that the Essenes substituted their Holy Meal before noon for the second period of prayer.

It is well known that the Jews when they prayed, if they were outside their native land, turned their faces toward Jerusalem as prayers were said. Of Daniel these words are recorded:

> ". . . he went into his house; (now his windows were open . . . toward Jerusalem;) and he kneeled upon his knees three times a day, and prayed, and gave thanks before his God, as he did aforetime." (Daniel 6:10.)

The Essenes did not face Jerusalem when they prayed but rather turned eastward whence came the light of the sun, which was apparently to them a symbol of God. In no sense were they worshiping the sun, as some have alleged, but having seen life in terms of light and darkness it would be natural to connect a God of light with the physical source of light. Although there is no proof of this, it seems to be quite probable that these same Essenes faced the setting sun in the west at vesper time.

Here the Qumran material does in fact clarify a point which has puzzled students for many years. While the Jews faced Jerusalem when they prayed, Christians, like the Essenes, faced the east. The followers of Jesus were no more worshiping the sun than were the Essenes, since the symbolism of the two groups in this instance was almost identical. The orientation for prayer then was in all probability a direct borrowing from Essenism by the early Church!

Early Church architecture was also oriented eastward, but the reason for it had been a puzzle. It seems that in this case there was recognizable influence from Qumran upon the Christian community. It may well be that sunrise had an added attraction to the Christians because of the resurrection at dawn on the first day of the week. Light and darkness were thus interwoven with the fabric of faith and found their expression at once in the position for prayer and in the orientation of early church buildings.

In summary, it is possible to trace a similarity in form between the two sacraments of the two communities. Baptism and the Lord's Supper as celebrated in the Church, however, had a completely different meaning and a variant historical development. It is entirely possible that in both cases the two communities were not dependent on each other but drew rather from a common source. In the case of orientation for daily prayer the situation is different; here a borrowing from the Essenes by the Church is not only feasible but quite apparent. Yet in all these cases there is strong reason to conclude that some direct as well as indirect contact occurred between the two communions.

5.   Organization and Nature of the Two Communities

MUCH HAS BEEN WRITTEN about organizational affinities of the Qumran community with the Christian Church. Upon discovering that the Essenes were ruled by twelve elders, some investigators immediately drew the unwarranted conclusion that at this point the form of Christian community had been dictated by Essene organizational structure. In addition, there were three priests in the hierarchy who have frequently been compared with the three intimates of Jesus: Peter, James, and John. Moreover, other apparent similarities have been pressed beyond all reason in a wild rush to prove a point or to find a historical source for some New Testament or early Church institution.

It is axiomatic in Protestant New Testament studies that no well-thought-out, well-ordered organization in the early Church existed except that which was inherited from Hebrew communal life, out of which Christianity sprang. It seems obvious that Jesus chose twelve apostles largely because there had been twelve tribes of Israel. Since this was the people of the New Covenant, the New Israel of faith, it continued to exist with an organization not of twelve tribes but of twelve apostles. In fact, the Master made the promise to His apostles: "Verily I say unto you, that ye who have followed me, in the regeneration when the Son of man shall sit on the throne of his glory, ye also shall sit upon twelve thrones, judging the twelve tribes of Israel." (Matthew 19:28.)

When Jesus was no longer visibly present with His disciples, there was no blueprint for organization because He had devised none. Only eleven men remained banded together after Judas, who had chosen the role of traitor, met with suicidal death and was buried in Akeldama. Just before the ascension from Olivet, these anxious words were exchanged between the Living Master and His vexed apostles:

Apostles: "Lord, dost thou at this time restore the
             kingdom to Israel?"
Jesus: "It is not for you to know times or seasons,
             which the Father hath set within his own
             authority." [1]

After the ascension the exact temporal schedule of the coming Kingdom was still a matter of uncertainty; hence the apostles with others, after prayer, held an election. To these Christian Jews it was unthinkable that the New Israel might be restored before the full complement of twelve apostles had been revived. Lots were cast between two men, Barsabbas and Matthias, and the latter was designated as the twelfth apostle of the Church. Only after the choice of Matthias had been made was the Church ready organization-wise for the consummation of the Kingdom.

Except for this incident, little is heard about the place of the Twelve in the Church. In fact, the persecution which began with the stoning of Stephen caused many to disperse, making a formal directorship of the Twelve impossible. It can be categorically stated that the position of the twelve apostles in the early Church was based not on any plan of organization but solely on their close association with Jesus in the days of His flesh. Certainly James the brother of Jesus gained great prominence in the Church, as did Paul and others who were not among the twelve apostles.

It is obvious that the twelve apostles of the Church and the twelve elders of Qumran were chosen in both cases because each community understood itself as a people of a new covenant, the New Israel. This fact of faith on the part of the Church is clearly stated in I Peter 2:9:

> "But ye are an elect race, a royal priesthood, a holy nation, a people for God's own possession, that ye may show forth the excellencies of him who called you out of darkness into his marvellous light . . ."

Qumran's inhabitants could have used these same words with respect to their own community since the membership of the group was thought to be Israel of the Spirit. For this reason and this reason alone, each continued the twelve-tribe order which was drawn from the distant past. From that point of origin, however, the similarity between the two ceases. In Qumran the twelve-man group shared the leadership with three priests. But there were none in the early Church because Christians recognized in Christ the one effective and permanent Mediator. The Essene Council of twelve was, in fact, a supreme ruling authority in a closely knit, well-organized society consisting of sedentary groups, dwelling in various places, withdrawn from the world. That tight organization is described in the *Manual*:

> There shall be in the council of the community twelve men, and there shall be three priests who are perfect in all that has been revealed of the whole law, to practice truth and righteousness and justice and loyal love and walking humbly each with his neighbor, to preserve

faithfulness in the land with sustained purpose and a
broken spirit, and to make amends for iniquity by the
practice of justice and the distress of tribulation, and
to walk with all by the standard of truth and by the
regulation of the time.[2]

In the Church no indication is given that the apostles ever
became in any sense a formal ruling body who passed on
questions of any kind. Moreover, machinery was not devised
to replace an apostle in his "official" capacity upon death.
Whereas Qumran was a settled group, satisfied to let the
world go by, the Church was ever in flux, restlessly moving
out to proclaim the good news of Christ to all men—a difference inevitably reflected in organizational structure.

When the apostles began to grow old and pass from the
scene, elders and bishops arose who served the Church in
local areas, but the number was far in excess of twelve.

Paul and his colleagues are said to have appointed elders
in the churches of Asia Minor as the local rulers of the congregation. (Acts 14:23.) Whether the office was simply filled
by the venerable men of a community, or was in fact an
office to which any might be called who had the right quali-
fications, is not certain. Again there is no question here
about the origin of the office being little more than an extension of a form which dates back to Moses. Moreover, bishop
and elder in this early stage of Christianity were probably
synonymous terms for the same office. A passage in the
Epistle to Titus gives this suggestion a high degree of
probability:

"For this cause left I thee in Crete, that thou shouldest
set in order the things that were wanting, and appoint
elders in every city, as I gave thee charge; if any man

is blameless, the husband of one wife, having children
that believe, who are not accused of riot or unruly.
For the bishop must be blameless, as God's steward."
(Titus 1:5-7a.)

At this preliminary stage of the Church's institutional development, the monarchical aspect of the bishop's duties had
not really begun. It appears that the overseer or bishop at
Qumran was more a ruler of his group than was his counter-
part among New Testament Christians. Some contact between the two offices is possible, and there is a probability
that Essene influence was brought to bear on the development of the episcopacy at a later stage. Beyond that, hardly
any genuine organizational affinity with the Church has
been found.

The elders from many areas gathered to decide theological
issues for the Church in general, whose domain had become
widespread. In such meetings, they appear to share a like
status with the apostles. Jerusalem's conference (Acts 15)
was made up of the apostles and elders who gathered
to consider the matter of the Judaizing question, that is to
say, whether Christians in order to be admitted to the
Church would be required to undergo the formal rites of
Judaism. No such regional conference has been discovered
in the records of the Essenes.

This aspect of our subject could be carried on at some
length, but suffice it to say that the organization of the two
communities was basically different because their aims were
fundamentally at variance. One group was a tight little
colony which had withdrawn from the world, in which it
professed to have no further interest. The foremost problem
for the Essenes was to sustain life in a well-ordered com-

munity, indoctrinating only those who sought them out for instruction, while preserving in writing the Scriptures and secrets of their heritage. On the other hand, Christians were a society, though not of the world, certainly in the midst of the world. Their great commission was to go into all the world to witness to the gospel of Christ and to increase the citizenship of the New Israel of faith. Except for incidental similarities, the organizations were of necessity poles apart. Paul in his letters both to the Ephesians and to the Corinthians showed that the offices of service in the Church had been multiplied many fold. Among those listed are apostles, prophets, evangelists, pastors, teachers, miracle workers, healers, governors, and speakers with unknown tongues. (See I Corinthians 12:28-31; Ephesians 4:12.) To fulfill a complicated task, the organization of the Church quickly became multiform in so far as offices were concerned. But the office of deacon, held in honor in the early Church, was not specifically designated among the Essene devotees at the Dead Sea.

It may then be said in summary that the Church functioning in the world was at once more complicated, diverse, and changing than was the sect of Qumran. Similarities such as exist must be understood as coincident with the common Hebrew background out of which both groups arose.

In addition to the organizational contact seen in the twelve-man supreme councils of each group, there is also said to be similarity in the attitude of the Qumran sect and the Church concerning the possession of private property. The *Manual of Discipline* categorically forbids the owning of property in these unmistakable terms:

And all who have offered themselves for his truth shall

> bring all their knowledge and strength and wealth into
> the community of God . . .[3]

When the novitiate was in process of becoming a full-fledged
member of the brotherhood, at the end of one year "His
wealth and his wages shall be put at the disposal of the man
who has supervision over the wages of the many, and he
shall enter it in the account at his disposal but shall not
spend it for the many." After successful completion of the
last year of preparation, the novitiate is given the following privileges:

> If the lot determines that he is to be admitted to the
> community, he shall be registered in the order of his
> position among his brethren, for law and for judgment
> and for the sacred food and for the sharing of his prop-
> erty . . .[4]

Every Christian is familiar with the parallel development
in the New Testament Church as reflected in the records
of Acts:

> "And all that believed were together, and had all things
> common; and they sold their possessions and goods,
> and parted them to all, according as any man had need."
> (Acts 2:44-45.)

There was no definite regulation which made pooling of
property mandatory in the Church as there evidently was
among the Essenes, nor was there any Christian doctrine
comparable to the idea that possessions are evil. Unity of the
Spirit and of faith in the Church made it logical for believers
to share their wealth with the less fortunate who had become brothers in Christ, hence the communalistic move-

ment gained real momentum with indirect pressure being brought to bear on all the membership to conform to the pattern. Ananias and Sapphira wanted the approval of the group without making the necessary sacrifice of their holdings. Their tragic demise resulted. (See Acts 4:32–5:11.)

One must be careful not to push this parallel beyond the limits which the facts allow. Joining a community in the desert, separating oneself from the world of commerce and private possession, was one thing; but giving up property in the ordinary business of living, that others might not suffer want, was quite another. The initiate in the Qumran sect gained security with his contribution of material resources for which he would have no further use. In other words, giving up possessions was part of the act of separating oneself from the world and becoming a member of the brotherhood.

Among Christians, there developed a spontaneous desire to share with those to whom they had been drawn by a common faith in Jesus Christ. No security of a desert retreat was purchased thereby, nor was any permanent separation from the wicked world of commerce promised. Nevertheless, a definite contact between the two communions in respect to one facet of motivation must be recognized. Christian and Essene alike were made more willing to part with possessions because each felt that the end of the age was near. With the coming of God's Kingdom, physical property would be a thing of no value. Except for that kindred motivation, the matter of common property in the Church and at Qumran appears to have arisen out of two separate sets of circumstances.

Having considered briefly certain organizational aspects of these two spiritual communities which developed contemporaneously, it would be well for the reader to understand that the groups were basically similar in their understanding of themselves. The Essene community did in fact withdraw from the world in a very literal, physical sense, but the Church no less withdrew from that same world, though not physically. Paul enjoined Christians as follows:

> "Come ye out from among them, and be ye separate,
>   saith the Lord,
> And touch no unclean thing;
> And I will receive you,
> And will be to you a Father,
> And ye shall be to me sons and daughters."
> (II Corinthians 6:17-18.)

The Apostle to the Gentiles chided these same Corinthian Christians for taking to civil court cases of dispute among themselves which, he maintained, should have been decided in their midst. They were *de facto* a new kingdom which by the magnetic force of its life sought to lift the world into the same citizenship of faith and love. Jesus spoke of the Church as being in the world but not of the world, thus recognizing a real sense of separation from the world on the part of His followers. (See John 17:14.)

There is this similarity in these two orders' concepts of their existence as separate from the world, which made their duties to each other in the new society more exacting than their obligation to the world in general. In addition both felt they possessed secrets which were forbidden ordinary men. The Essene promised to resist to the death the devolvement of any of the esoteric material which was the prize possession of his group. This was a matter of sheer defense from profanation which would result should the world by stealth capture these sacred truths. Undoubtedly, such an attitude is but one additional reason for careful concealment of the scrolls in caves and elsewhere prior to the destruction of the center in A.D. 68. Disciples, as is apparent in Matthew 13, were amazed to find that Jesus couched His teachings in parables so that the populace might not understand His meaning. Admittedly, this is an interpretation of the event which may be late. Whether or not this is original or later does not alter the fact that the Church felt that the outsider could not understand the meaning of Christian faith. However, there was no attempt to protect the faith. On the contrary, the Church was anxious for the non-believer to obtain the eyes of faith wherewith he could discern clearly the meaning of Christ. In one case, the secret could be known only by commitment to a desert band with an oath to keep the doctrine secret, whereas in the other the non-believer needed but to have faith and the secret of Christ's full meaning would be revealed. Here again the parallel was more apparent than real.

Both groups celebrated their oneness and their separateness in the Holy Meal to which only members might come, a fact with which we dealt in the previous chapter. Within the group there was a spirit of kindred love which was not expected to find its fullest expression outside. Even so, the Essenes demanded of their members that they hate those outside, while the Christian ethic to love one's enemies is well known as a unique feature of Jesus' message. Indeed, Jesus could well have had scornful reference to separatist sects such as the Qumran enclave when He said:

"For if ye love them that love you, what reward have ye? do not even the publicans the same? And if ye salute

your brethren only, what do ye more than others? do
not even the Gentiles the same?" (Matthew 5:46-47.)

Unity and a sense of separation never permitted Christian
to hate the outsider or son of darkness, but rather through
love constrained them to seek by every means to draw him
into the family of God.

Within the two communities there was a very striking
resemblance in the way an offending brother was to be
treated. In both groups, a desire to restore to fellowship,
not to condemn to excommunication, can be easily detected.
In Matthew 18:15-17, this method of approach is given by
Christ to His followers:

> "And if thy brother sin against thee, go, show him his
> fault between thee and him alone: if he hear thee, thou
> hast gained thy brother. But if he hear thee not, take
> with thee one or two more, that at the mouth of two
> witnesses or three every word may be established. And
> if he refuse to hear them, tell it unto the church: and
> if he refuse to hear the church also, let him be unto thee
> as the Gentile and the publican."

The parallel is so very close that it should be sufficient to
quote the two passages without comment. In the *Manual of
Discipline*, the following approach is ordered:

> One shall not speak to his brother in anger or in re-
> sentment, or with a stiff neck or a hard heart or a wicked
> spirit; one shall not hate him in the folly of his heart.
> In his days he shall reprove him and shall not bring
> upon him iniquity; and also a man shall not bring against
> his neighbor a word before the masters [i.e., many]
> without having rebuked him before witnesses.[5]

Apparently it was incumbent upon Essene and Christian alike when he found a brother who had done wrong to give a personal reminder in private. Should that fail to bring the desired result, a rebuke in the presence of witnesses was prescribed. When the offender continued obdurate, the case was brought before the whole community for judgment.

While the point we have just discussed may prove to be one of the closest affinities betwixt Christianity and Essenism, the next facet of life, namely, the matter of rank, shows the two groups to be diametrically opposite. The Gospels record that Jesus made a point of teaching that consciousness of and desire for rank was contrary to the Christian ideal. Service was the key to greatness which could never be replaced by a sense of position. (Mark 9:34-37.) The Master drove home this lesson to two of His apostles who wished to sit beside Him in the coming glory. (Matthew 20:20-28.) Jesus further exhorted His disciples not to seek the prominent place lest they should be demoted to a more lowly position in the course of a feast. (Luke 14:7-11.) It is proper to draw the conclusion that there was in the early Christian movement an antipathy to any system of rank or privilege. Not so among the Essenes!

As we have already indicated, there was a place for each man in the Essene family and he was expected to know that place and stay in it. A key statement to that effect is given early in the *Manual of Discipline*:

> And none shall be abased below his appointed position or exalted above his allotted place; for they shall all be in true community and good humility and loyal love and righteous thought, each for his fellow in the holy council, and they shall be sons of the eternal assembly.[6]

The idea of rank carried over into the matter of seating positions when the group met as well as in the matter of processional order.

> This is the order for the session of the masters [i.e., many], each in his position. The priests be seated first and the elders second; then all the rest of the people shall be seated, each in his position.[7]

Heavy penalties attended any breach of this code for conduct among the Essene sect.

Stratification of position was not permanent since there appears to have been an annual promotion day among the Qumran inhabitants:

> . . . so that they shall have an investigation of their spirits and their works year by year, so as to elevate each one according to his understanding and the perfection of his way or put him back according to his perversions, so that each one may reprove his neighbor in truth and humility and loyal love for each one.[8]

In this instance, the two streams of tradition diverged and two very different attitudes resulted.

A careful look at the organization and nature of the community reveals that both, growing out of the Israel idea, carried out the number twelve in organization. For the Church, however, the apostles were never permanent nor were they a formal group in any sense of the word. The probability is that each community drew from a common source and neither was dependent on the other so far as this aspect of life was concerned. In the matter of possession of private property, the reason behind the action of the Church and the Essene sect could hardly have been more different.

Likewise, the separation from the world in each group was different not only in degree but also in kind. Within the community, treatment of and attitude toward a wayward brother was remarkably similar; but in the matter of rank the two served diametrically opposing ideals. With respect to organization, there was little direct influence from Qumran to the Church, not much indirect borrowing, some drawing from common sources, and very much independent development according to need.

6. from Darkness to Light

IDEAS HAVE NO BOUNDS and brook no barriers. We know that the canon of Scripture for the Church had not been finally set; nor for that matter had it been for Judaism at this juncture of history, and interchange of ideas was quite free, with none of the constraint later laid upon them by Church and synagogue alike. Such books as Enoch, the Book of Jubilees, and possibly part of the Book of the Twelve Patriarchs, all of which were produced in this period (about 200 B.C.-A.D. 68) might well have been composed at Qumran. That these works were used by the early Christian Church and their influences felt in Christian literature is well known to all who have made a brief investigation of the subject. It would be quickly pointed out, however, that borrowing from a literary work does not necessarily imply doctrinal dependence.

For many decades New Testament scholars have recognized in the writings of John and Paul a tendency toward understanding the spiritual world as dualistic in make-up (that is, two basic forces at work). Judaism, out of which both men arose, was patently monotheistic (that is, only one major, primary force), hence any idea of two co-equal deities struggling for supremacy was for them out of the question. Doubtless the original idea-loan came from Zoroastrianism in which the basic struggle did occur between the forces of evil and the forces of good. In Zoroastrianism, however, the conflict involved two full-grown gods, an idea which, as we have already indicated, would have been unacceptable in the Judaeo-Christian context. Some mediating position was sought between the pure dualism of Zoroastrianism and the more subdued dualism of the early Christian movement. Until the discovery of Qumran Cave I with its *Manual of Discipline* the gap could be filled only by theories, never by proven fact.

In several of the documents the expressions "sons of darkness" and "sons of light" are used, but only in the *Manual of Discipline* and perhaps in material yet to appear is found the basic creedal substructure.

He [God] created man to have dominion over the world and made for him two spirits, that he might walk by them until the appointed time of his visitation; they are the spirits of truth and of error. In the abode of light are the origins of truth, and from the source of darkness are the origins of error. In the hand of the prince of lights is dominion over all sons of righteousness; in the ways of light they walk. And in the hand of the angel of darkness is all dominion over the sons of error; and in the ways of darkness they walk. And by the angel of darkness is the straying of all the sons of righteousness, and all their sins and their iniquities and their guilt, and the transgressions of their works in his dominion, according to the mysteries of God, until his time, and all their afflictions and the appointed times of their distress in the dominion of his enmity. And all the spirits of his lot try to make the sons of light stumble; but the God of Israel and his angel of truth have helped all the sons of light. For he created the spirits of light and of darkness, and upon them he founded every work and upon their ways every service.

One of the spirits God loves for all the ages of eternity, and with all its deeds is pleased forever; as for the other, he abhors its company, and all its ways he hates forever.[1]

Thus in one paragraph the problem of evil is squarely faced and the basis for dualism in a monotheistic context is clearly explained. One God created two spirits and ordained the extent to which the struggle between them was to be carried, with the promise that He would one day annihilate the spirit of darkness, which He hated, and establish the spirit of light, for which He had eternal affection. All the human family is divided into two groups.

> In these two spirits are the origins of all the sons of man, and in their divisions all the hosts of men have their inheritance in their generations. In the ways of the two spirits men walk. And all the performance of their works is in their two divisions, according to each man's inheritance, whether much or little, for all the periods of eternity. For God has established the two spirits in equal measure until the last period, and has put eternal enmity between their divisions. An abomination to truth are deeds of error, and an abomination to error are all ways of truth. And contentious jealousy is on all their judgments, for they do not walk together.[2]

This cosmic struggle which found expression on every level of life happily moved toward the promised conclusion at the end of time.

> Thus far the spirits of truth and of error struggle in the heart of a man; they walk in wisdom and folly; and according to each man's inheritance in truth he does right, and so he hates error; but according to his pos-

session in the lot of error he does wickedly in it, and so he abhors truth. For an equal measure God has established the two spirits until the period which has been decreed and the making new; and he knows the performance of their works for all the periods of eternity. And he causes the sons of men to inherit them, that they may know good and evil, making the lots fall for every living man according to his spirit in the world until the time of visitation.[3]

Thus the dualism of Qumran, though creating problems of its own design, dealt very simply with the origin of evil and the struggle which was inherent in life itself.

This same struggle between good and evil is manifested in numerous passages of the New Testament. In a very dramatic and well-known passage the Apostle Paul wrote to the church of Ephesus explaining a phase of life which had presented a problem of no small importance to them.

"For our wrestling is not against flesh and blood, but against the principalities, against the powers, against the world-rulers of this darkness, against the spiritual hosts of wickedness in the heavenly places." (Ephesians 6:12.)

Paul refers to the sons of disobedience (Ephesians 2:2), while speaking of Christians as the "children of light" who should have no fellowship with the forces of darkness (Ephesians 5:7-12). One must agree that these passages reflect more than a common atmosphere, utilizing as they also do a common store not only of words but of ideas. Another striking passage in Paul's writings which is expressed in these same terms is addressed to the Romans.

"The night is far spent, and the day is at hand: let us

therefore cast off the works of darkness, and let us put
on the armor of light." (Romans 13:12.)

Verbal similarities also appear in Colossians where Christians are described as the saints of light who have been de-
livered out of the power of darkness into God's Kingdom of
love (Colossians 1:12-13) and in II Corinthians where light
is connected with the knowledge of God (II Corinthians
4:4).

The most astonishing parallel is to be found in the inner
spiritual struggle which Paul experienced and recorded in
his Epistle to the Romans:

> "For the good which I would I do not: but the evil
> which I would not, that I practise. But if what I would
> not, that I do, it is no more I that do it, but sin which
> dwelleth in me. I find then the law, that, to me who
> would do good, evil is present. For I delight in the
> law of God after the inward man: but I see a different
> law in my members, warring against the law of my
> mind, and bringing me into captivity under the law
> of sin which is in my members." (Romans 7:19-23.)

Doubtless the idea of a good impulse and a bad impulse in
every person was carried over by Paul from his rabbinical
training in Judaism, yet, in spite of that fact, the basic concept is closely akin to the Qumran doctrine of possession by
evil and good. Paul saw the evil desire in his own heart in
much the same terms as the Essenes who believed that the
forces of evil were evermore trying to trip the sons of light.
Kuhn's thesis that "temptation" in the New Testament should
be understood as the onslaught of darkness against the sons
of light must be accepted.

In Luke a revealing word of our Lord is couched in these terms:

> ". . . the sons of this world are for their own generation wiser than the sons of the light." (Luke 16:8.)

It is undeniable that Jesus on this occasion applied these terms, so familiar in the Qumran literature, to Christians and non-Christians. Upon His arrest Jesus explained the power and authority of those who imprisoned Him as follows:

> "When I was daily with you in the temple, ye stretched not forth your hands against me: but this is your hour, and the power of darkness." (Luke 22:53.)

Jesus knew the terminology of the Essene sect and apparently His audiences did also. Furthermore He was not at all reluctant to use such figures as a means of expressing the good news which was His to proclaim and explain.

As has been recognized from the outset, it is the Gospel of John which apparently has on it the deepest imprint of Essenism, at least so far as this light-darkness motif is concerned. In the prologue to that Gospel, one reads that "the light shineth in the darkness; and the darkness apprehended it not." (John 1:5.) John the Baptist in the same chapter was described as not the true light, after which the writer explained the character and purpose of the true light of whom John was the immediate forerunner.

> "There was the true light, even the light which lighteth every man, coming into the world." (John 1:9.)

Later Jesus revealed that He was in fact the light of the

world (John 8:12), a statement which was made even more definite in chapter 9:

> "When I am in the world, I am the light of the world."
> (John 9:5.)

The great climax of struggle in John was reached in chapter 12 when Jesus clearly explained His mission in terms of light and darkness.

> "I am come a light into the world, that whosoever believeth on me may not abide in the darkness." (John 12:46.)

Yet in this same context the struggle for the moment had seemingly turned against Jesus, which caused Him to say:

> "I will no more speak much with you, for the prince
> of the world cometh: and he hath nothing in me . . ."
> (John 14:30.)

Christ took the place of the spirit of light which was mentioned in the *Manual*, Himself being the Light of the World. His mission was to guide men from darkness to light. In this purpose He was opposed by one whom the writer called the ruler of this world instead of describing that figure in the same highly personalized way that Qumran literature did. That struggle was in process of being won by Christ, who was the light which the darkness could not put out. The victory of the light was signaled in at least two passages:

> "Now is the judgment of this world: now shall the
> prince of this world be cast out." (John 12:31.)

". . . the prince of this world hath been judged." (John 16:11.)

In this respect, therefore, the Christian concept of the struggle is different from that expressed by the Essene group. Essenes expected the two forces to continue equal until the end-time when God would destroy darkness. On the other hand, early Christians believed that the darkness which could not overcome Christ (John 1:5) was already beginning to pass away, since the prince of this world had been overcome by Christ.

For the Essenes the victory awaited the end-time when cherished spiritual ambitions of the community would be fulfilled. At the Last Day the Essenes expected to march out in Holy War against the heathen in the name of God— this as over against Jesus' remark that His Kingdom was not of this world; hence His disciples would not engage in physical combat. (John 18:36.) The victory which Jesus won in the death-resurrection event caused the darkness to pass away for all who by faith accepted His victory as their own personal conquest. By allying oneself with the Light of the World, that victory is shared here and now, not alone in some far-off tomorrow. For the Essene this was a hope dimly seen, whereas for the Christian the victory over darkness was by faith already a precious possession.

This brings the subject up to the edge of a field which we shall discuss at some length later, namely the consummation of this age. At this juncture a clear understanding of what this meant to the life and attitude of the two groups is needed. One gazed hopefully ahead for the coming Kingdom, the other rejoiced in the possession of the victory of light and looked forward to the increase of that victory in life and history. Whereas the Kingdom was coming for the Essene, the Christian from earliest times believed it had come in Christ, was coming in the Church, and would be fulfilled at some future time. As the Christian entered the struggle, having known the personal victory of faith, he was sustained by the absolute assurance that ultimate victory would be attained.

The reader might be curious to know how a person became a son of darkness or a son of light in each community. Apparently by the grace of God some were elected to membership in the Essene group, thus becoming sons of light. So far as can be discerned, the natural inclination of man was to be a son of darkness, with a stubborn unwillingness to follow the will of the Almighty being the chief characteristic of those who loved darkness rather than light. Jesus likewise held that men loved darkness because their deeds were evil. He took as His mission the persuasion of the sons of darkness to walk in the light of life. Refusing this, they were condemned to the darkness from which they had failed to emerge. Henceforth they would have no fellowship with Christ or with the children of light. The differences in development of what certainly must have been a basic idea with both groups are so apparent as to make further comment superfluous.

It is a simple matter of logical deduction to conclude that the sons of light at Qumran were co-extensive with the community membership resident on the desert plateau. Joining the community, learning the peculiar interpretation of the Law and obeying it, transformed an individual into a son of light. What were the characteristics of these righteous men? What quality did their life possess?

These are the counsels of the Spirit for the sons of the
truth of the world and the visitation of all who walk
by it, for healing and abundance of peace in length
of days, and bringing forth seed, with all eternal bless-
ings and everlasting joy in the life of eternity, and a
crown of glory with raiment of majesty in everlasting
light.[5]

Paul described the Christian life when he wrote that the
fruit of the Spirit is love, joy, and peace (Galatians 5:22);
he promised in the name of Christ a crown of glory and
eternal life as well. The ideals for the good and faithful man
held by both communities do in a measure converge.

Furthermore, the pictures of the unbeliever recorded on
the one hand in the Essene *Manual* and on the other by the
Apostle to the Gentiles are even more similar:

But to the spirit of error belong greediness, slackness
of hands in the service of righteousness, wickedness and
falsehood, pride and haughtiness, lying and deceit, cru-
elty and great impiety, quickness to anger and abundance of folly and proud jealousy, abominable works in
the spirit of fornication and ways of defilement in the
service of uncleanness, and a blasphemous tongue,
blindness of eyes and dullness of ears, stiffness of neck
and hardness of heart, walking in all the ways of darkness and evil cunning.[6]

How like an echo are the words of Galatians 5:19-21a:

"Now the works of the flesh are manifest, which are
these: fornication, uncleanness, lasciviousness, idolatry,
sorcery, enmities, strife, jealousies, wraths, factions, divi-
sions, parties, envyings, drunkenness, revellings, and
such like . . ."

That the ideal picture of the good man and the description of the evil were all but identical is an undeniable fact and indicates that direct influence ideologically was brought to bear on the early Church by the Essenes.

In the expression of spiritual truth figures of speech are necessarily employed; these may come from a wide variety of sources. Since therefore the light-darkness motif is found both in the Qumran literature and in the New Testament, it is safe to assume that it began in its present form with the Essenes. The development of the figure in Christianity was different because Light became incarnate and darkness was overcome by the victory of the Cross. Even so, for adequate expression of the new life in Christ which was also a matter of struggle, Christians borrowed the figure and refashioned it to their own needs. In this instance the Church is most indebted to the Essenes but in no sense dependent upon nor secondary to them in religious content.

7. Creeds in Common?

OFTENTIMES an apparent verbal similarity in two pieces of literature can cause much excitement when first discovered, and can result in the most outlandish theories concerning the origins of the two pieces. This is especially true when one is dealing with the era and the ideological background out of which the Christian movement began. It is understandable that scholars, Sunday school teachers, preachers, and the professional intellectual should have had a field day when a little knowledge of the scrolls material became available.

The Christian Church has long recognized that the movement which Jesus began and which His followers developed was to some extent an extension of the Hebrew faith wrought out in the Old Testament. In fact, the Church met in the synagogue and frequented the Temple. Its membership was made up primarily of Jews who believed that Jesus was the Messiah. Ideas and vocabulary for the new faith were drawn largely from the background of Jewish religion and life of earlier and contemporary times. There were, however, radical shifts made by Jesus and His disciples from certain positions of practice within contemporary Judaism. It was in this realm that the average Christian felt secure in the uniqueness and newness of the faith. With the coming of the Messiah some new elements had been added to old ones and a different direction had been plotted.

In the light of the above situation it was with some sense of shock that Christians read this passage from the *Thanksgiving Psalms* of the Essenes:

> I know that righteousness does not belong to a man,
> nor to a son of man blamelessness of conduct;
> to the Most High God belong all works of righteousness.
> A man's way is not established
> except by the spirit which God created for him,
> to make blameless a way for the sons of man,
> that they may know all his works
> in the might of his power and the greatness of his mercy
> to all the sons of his good pleasure.[1]

This passage had in it the astonishing suggestion that the Essenes were in fact the originators of the doctrine of salvation by faith and Christians were simply their imitators. To show how striking is the surface similarity two passages from Paul's writings will suffice:

> "But now apart from the law a righteousness of God hath been manifested, being witnessed by the law and the prophets; even the righteousness of God through faith in Jesus Christ unto all them that believe; for there is no distinction; for all have sinned, and fall short of the glory of God; being justified freely by his grace through the redemption that is in Christ Jesus . . ."
> (Romans 3:21-24.)

> "We being Jews by nature, and not sinners of the Gentiles, yet knowing that a man is not justified by the works of the law but through faith in Jesus Christ . . ."
> (Galatians 2:15-16a.)

Behind both passages there is apparently the same view as that which can be detected in a number of places in Essene literature. The sect at Qumran was quite blunt about the fact that its ritual baths were incapable of accomplishing regeneration in and of themselves. Righteousness was God's gift; at least this seems to be so if we have read correctly the material at hand.

Even more astonishing than the fact that righteousness was not a quality which a man deserved or purchased, but rather a divine gift, is the intimation that salvation was by faith in the Teacher of Righteousness. This conclusion is certainly logically based on the interpretation of a familiar passage in the *Habakkuk Commentary:*

> *But the righteous shall live by his faith.* This means all the doers of the law in the house of Judah, whom God will rescue from the house of judgment because of their labor and their faith in the teacher of righteousness.[2]

Immediately upon reading these provocative words many persons, from the specialist in New Testament studies to the ordinary reader, began to see a parallel between salvation by faith in the Teacher of Righteousness among the Essenes and salvation by faith in Jesus among Christians. In a long discourse on salvation by faith written to the Galatians, Paul used this same passage from Habakkuk as his proof text:

> "Now that no man is justified by the law before God, is evident: for, The righteous shall live by faith; and the law is not of faith; but, He that doeth them shall live in them." (Galatians 3:11-12.)

The picture seemed to be complete with sections from the latter psalms of the *Manual of Discipline,* only a sample of which shall be presented here:

As for me, if I slip,
the steadfast love of God is my salvation forever;
and if I stumble in the iniquity of flesh,
my vindication in the righteousness of God will stand
    to eternity.[3]

This surface parallel dissolves and disappears under closer scrutiny. Salvation by faith in the Teacher of Righteousness had a completely different meaning from what was described by salvation through faith in Jesus Christ. In fact, the Teacher of Righteousness taught that salvation came by adherence to the Law in a law community. Keeping apart from the world, swearing allegiance to the Law of Moses, participating in the life and knowledge of the community, was in fact the way of salvation. Faith in the Teacher of Righteousness meant acceptance of what he stood for and adherence to the principles which he laid down as the true ways of righteousness and justice. It is quite correct to say that the salvation by personal faith in this figure actually amounted to salvation by works of law which Paul so desperately denied and detested.

We need not dwell long on the fact that Jesus radically revised a particularistic interpretation of the Law, with its adherence to the minutest rule, and enunciated the broad motivational basis for the good life in the memorable combination of two Old Testament passages, Deuteronomy 6:5 and Leviticus 19:18:

> "Thou shalt love the Lord thy God with all thy heart, and with all thy soul, and with all thy mind. . . . Thou shalt love thy neighbor as thyself. On these two commandments the whole law hangeth, and the prophets." (Matthew 22:37-40.)

While Essenism multiplied rules and regulations, setting liturgies and practices on the basis of the Law, building in this way a law community, the Master of the Christians was reducing legalism to the basic motivation, presenting love as the totality of God's desire.

A cursory reading of Paul's Epistles reveals a strong antipathy to any doctrine of salvation by works of law following precepts or regulations drawn out of the Mosaic code. Countless passages might be presented in support of this conclusion, but one should be enough to clarify the basic idea:

> ". . . by grace have ye been saved through faith; and that not of yourselves, it is the gift of God; not of works, that no man should glory." (Ephesians 2:8-9.)

Salvation as Paul understood it was not wrought by a faith in Jesus simply as a worthy teacher and good leader together with a willingness to follow His leading; redemption resulted when a man put his trust in the work which Christ accomplished in the death-resurrection event. The results of this cosmic event could be accrued to the believer personally by a simple affirmation of their spiritual validity. Life in Christ began for the believer when, through faith, he died unto sin that he might live unto righteousness. Symbolically the convert died with Christ and was raised to a new life, not in temporal extension alone but more in the new quality of life. The risen life in Christ could be attained by faith in the resurrected Lord whom God sent to redeem the world.

Although it would not be feasible or valuable to enter into an extended discussion of this elementary theology of the Christian faith, one more brief suggestion might prove helpful. Justification from God was a free gift of His grace, given to any who by faith were ready to accept it in humility. Law made man aware of his need for God's saving love—it was a schoolmaster which led to Christ. Regulations kept and deeds done were not the key to eternal life but constituted a thank-offering on the part of the believer for what God had fashioned in his life. No such approach to the good life, no like-minded doctrine, has yet been discovered in the Qumran scrolls and fragments.

The sovereignty of God was a major aspect of Qumran doctrine. He was the maker of all things, the giver of all gifts, and the director of the destinies of men. God was at the very center of life and history.

> There is none besides thee,
> and there is none with thee in strength;
> there is nothing over against thy glory,
> and thy power has no price.[4]

The Essenes recognized, as did the prologue to the Fourth Gospel, that God was the creator of all things and without Him nothing was made. It was clear to them that the Almighty created both the forces of good and the forces of evil, appointing a certain amount of time in which they might contend with each other, but that He also set a definite *terminus* to the tension which is the texture of life in this age.

Inherent in the strong emphasis on God's sovereign power was a doctrine of predestination which is more an atmosphere than a logical dogma. God has chosen the sons of the covenant for a holy remnant, but at the same time He has ordained that some should be the sons of darkness. That view amounts to double-predestination.

Needless to say, any group rooted in the Scriptures and the faith of the Hebrews would emphasize the sovereign power of God. To have done otherwise would have meant a clean break with a firmly established doctrine of long standing. Expressions concerning the sovereignty of God as they appeared among the Essenes and the Christians are but variant developments of a major theme of Old Testament religion. Both communities undoubtedly drew from the same source with neither being directly dependent on the other.

The Church and the Qumran community lived in the expectation that the Age would soon end, ushering in the Kingdom of God with power. Christians expected Jesus who had ascended from the earth to return in "clouds of glory" and establish the New Israel forever. Essenes looked for the advent of the Messiah whose presence would beget the same result. There is absolutely no evidence that the Teacher of Righteousness was Messiah who had been done to death, had risen, and would return in glory. Some scholars have been guilty of superimposing Christian doctrine on the Essene community without any objective data to support them. Too often the theory becomes its own proof, which is, to say the least, an invalid approach. Many groundless statements in the press and on radio have resulted from this unfortunate procedure. It is certain on the basis of evidence that the Essenes were looking for the first coming of Messiah with the advent of the New Age, as will be shown in the next chapter.

Paul and others in the early Church expected the glorious fulfillment of the Kingdom at any moment. To the Romans he wrote this explanation of the current scene:

> "And this, knowing the season, that already it is time for you to awake out of sleep: for now is salvation nearer to us than when we first believed. The night is far spent, and the day is at hand: let us therefore cast off the works of darkness, and let us put on the armor of light." (Romans 13:11-12.)

In the very practical field of marriage the great apostle had a word for those who might have plans for this aspect of living:

> "But this I say, brethren, the time is shortened, that henceforth both those that have wives may be as though they had none . . ." (I Corinthians 7:29.)

The book of Revelation, of course, was written in the shadow of this same expectation, as were the Epistle of James and the First Epistle of Peter.

The same framework was set about the life at Qumran. God had appointed a time when the age of tension would be done away; that time could not be far distant although the Essenes do not speak much of its being immediately at hand. That the temporal reckoning of both communities was inaccurate is a matter of record.

When the days were extended and the coming victory was put off, questions arose at Qumran as in the Church. Both groups needed to adapt to this shift in historical situation. For the Essenes the writer of the *Habakkuk Commentary* gave this explanation:

> And God told Habakkuk to write the things that were to come upon the last generation, but the con-summation of the period he did not make known to him. . . .
>
> *For still the vision is for an appointed time; it hastens to the period and does not lie.* This means that the last period extends over and above all that the prophets said; for the mysteries of God are marvelous. *If it tarries, wait for it, for it will surely come; it will not delay.* This means the men of truth, the doers of the law, whose hands do not grow slack from the service of the truth, when the last period is stretched out over them.[5]

The writer of II Peter faced this difficulty for the Christians, trying in chapter 3 to offset questions and taunts about the Second Coming. He reiterated that God's Kingdom would come as a thief in the night and the time was extended so that none should perish. Central to this attitude was the affirmation of II Peter 3:13:

> "But, according to his promise, we look for new heavens and a new earth, wherein dwelleth righteousness."

Actually an air of expectancy seems to have been a part of the attitude in many religious sects of the day, both Christian and Jewish. Qumran and the Church are then but two pieces in the pattern of the times, settling in their own peculiar way the extension of the consummation.

There are verbal affinities in the descriptions given in the scroll of the *War of the Sons of Light with the Sons of Darkness* on the one hand and the book of Revelation on the other. Both drew heavily from earlier Biblical apocalyptic literature, as well as from common sources in non-Biblical writings. Both recognized a season when God would allow evil to run rampant upon the earth and a time when He would utterly destroy that evil. The armies of God and the final battle are common property of the two groups, inherited from Judaism and the Hebrew faith. It would seem that Revelation represents a later refinement and crystallization of the same basic ideas which were expressed by the Essene sect. Here again, the divergencies far outweigh the similarities. The most that can be said until further study is done and further material is made available is that Essenism had breathed the same atmosphere.

Having spoken about formal creeds and ponderous ideas

of the two groups it would be well to turn to a basic kinship which is often overlooked. In the poetry of devotion there lived in Qumran the fires of genuine devotion and personal love for God. This facet of the Essene sect is beautifully expressed in one of the Thanksgiving Psalms:

> From my youth thou hast appeared to me in thy just wisdom,
> and with firm truth thou hast sustained me.
> With thy Holy Spirit thou dost delight me,
> and to this day thou dost lead me.
> Thy righteous rebuke is with my thoughts,
> and the guarding of thy peace to deliver my soul;
> abundance of pardon with my steps,
> and a multitude of mercies when thou dost enter into
>   judgment with me;
> and to old age thou wilt support me.
> For my father does not know me,
> and my mother against thee has forsaken me;
> but thou art a Father to all the sons of thy truth;
> thou rejoicest over them
> like her who has compassion on her sucking child;
> and like a foster father thou wilt sustain in thy bosom
> all that thou hast made.[6]

Here is personal devotion at its very finest.

The Church and Essenism developed in the same age and came out of the same general background. Facing similar problems in like circumstances, the two movements could not have been absolutely dissimilar in doctrine. One should never forget, however, that the development of the idea of salvation by faith in the Christian Church was utterly different in content from any creed of Qumran. So also it was with the doctrines of the Sovereignty of God and the Coming Age.

8. the Messiahs, the Teacher of Righteousness, and Jesus

THE EXPECTATION that God would send His anointed to redeem His people out of distress dates back at least to the time when Israel became disenchanted with the monarchy. Naturally the form in which the Messiah would appear was that of a king. He would fulfill the hopes and desires of Israel which ordinary monarchs had previously attempted without success. Ideally the king's office had been intended to represent God's rule on earth, with the ruler always being subservient and obedient to the higher divine will; but that ideal unhappily was not often near fulfillment in the parade of royalty across that part of history's stage which Israel occupied. A figure of a new David, drawn from an idealization of the real man, became the form for Messianic expectation and hope.

Another facet of this aspect of religion was the disillusionment with the priesthood which developed during the time when the heirs of the Maccabean Revolt pre-empted the priestly office. For some time the priesthood was defamed beyond measure, becoming little more than a pawn used by various factions in the struggle for power. It was only natural that these circumstances should cause pious folk to pray and hope for a priestly Messiah who would fulfill the office in its ideal sense.

In the midst of the Babylonian Exile (587-539 B.C.), and

thereafter, the people of Israel had entered into a period of frustration and suffering out of which had come the concept of the Suffering Servant. This was a fluid idea which could refer either to the nation Israel or to some individual; but in either case, the redemptive power of suffering had entered the picture. This definitely influenced the concept which emerged, especially in the development of the Christian faith.

Prior to the coming of the Messiah, a prophet would prepare the way; hence there were at least three phases to the expectation as it existed in inter-Testament times. A prophet, a priest, and a king were expected from God in the Messianic Age. In Jesus, these offices were merged.

Being a Jewish sect, the Essenes at Qumran were heirs of the same Messianic pattern as were the Christians. A chief reason for going into the desert, as stated above, was to prepare there a highway for the coming king. That preparation consisted largely of membership in a law community and obedience to the interpretation of the Law as taught within the brotherhood. At the end-time apparently the Messiah would appear and his coming would signal the conclusion of the struggle between light and darkness which God had ordained to be the nature of history.

In the *Damascus Document* reference is made to the Messiah of Aaron and Israel, but in the earlier *Manual of Discipline* text, the correct reading is "the Messiahs of Aaron and Israel." The Essenes expected two different Messiahs— one a priest of the Aaronic line and the other a king of David's lineage. The priestly aspect of the Qumran community cannot be overstated since it is well known that they understood themselves as the true descendants of Zadok, whose line was to be continued through them. It is highly unlikely that there was any merger of the Aaron and Israel Messiahs at Qumran, at least within the period which we know.

Jesus was accepted by the Church as the Messiah of God who combined in Himself all these multiple aspects of Jewish prophecy concerning God's anointed. In the eyes of the early Church He fulfilled the offices of prophet in teaching, priest in sacrificing Himself, and king over all the Church, indicating that the development of the idea had progressed further among Christians than among the Essenes. Jesus became King, but His Kingdom was not of this world. He gave no orders for war, and His followers were even forbidden to fight in His defense. His Kingdom was of the spirit and was only planted in the Incarnation; the harvest was to come with His second advent. In the interim between the Incarnation and the Second Coming He promised to send another divine person, the Holy Spirit, to direct the development of His Kingdom in the hearts and lives of men.

While Qumran looked expectantly for the Messiah, the Christian community built its faith around the fact that in Jesus Christ, God's appointed servant had already come. Indeed, this same Jesus had more than fulfilled the totality of Hebrew expectation by being the anointed, but beyond that He was God incarnate. The Christian idea of Jesus naturally developed far beyond its Hebrew origins and Essene contemporary thought. While Qumran waited, Christians rejoiced in a Messiah who had brought freedom from the power of sin and the reign of death. To see any more than a common origin of ideas between the groups is stretching evidence to the breaking point.

No single country can claim credit for making the scrolls a tabloid sensation, since scholars in at least three nations

have done just that. The device was quite simple and completely effective, creating a very definite sensation among
readers who were alarmed to learn that the Essene Teacher
of Righteousness was the original and Jesus was a poor copy
made more than a century later, clearly patterned after the
Essene prototype. So convincing was this line of reasoning
to those who produced it that soon conjecture became to
them solid fact. This discovery allegedly not only destroyed
the uniqueness of Christ but also called in question the
originality of His person. It was presumed in many places
that the Teacher of Righteousness underwent the same
death-resurrection experience and was expected to return
for judgment. The fact that there was no evidence for these
conclusions in no way hindered their proclamation.

Just who was the Teacher of Righteousness in the history
of the Essenes? He was in a very true sense the founder who
welded an otherwise amorphous group into a functioning
spiritual organism. In all probability the era of his ministry
was in the late second and early first centuries B.C. Accurate
identification of this person with some otherwise known historical figure is out of the question, even though many such
attempts have been and doubtless will continue to be made.
Whoever he was, the imprint of his work and personal character upon the Qumran community was so great that it
thought in terms of the Messiah as one who would himself
teach righteousness. This allusion has led some to the
erroneous conclusion that the Teacher of Righteousness was
Messiah.

Establishing the sect in Palestine was apparently not easy
because it invited persecution from the secular and spiritual
authorities of the day. Some wicked priest, whose name is
unknown, was represented as having wronged the Teacher

of Righteousness and as a result was consigned to destruction by God. A passage from the *Habakkuk Commentary* reflects the continued struggle between the Teacher of Righteousness and the wicked priest:

> *Woe to him who makes his neighbors drink, who pours out his wrath; yea, he has made them drunk, to gaze on their festivals!* This means the wicked priest, who persecuted the teacher of righteousness in order to confound him in the indignation of his wrath, wishing to banish him; and at the time of their festival of rest, the day of atonement, he appeared to them to confound them and to make them stumble on the day of fasting, their Sabbath of rest.[1]

How far persecution went and what form it took is a matter of pure conjecture. Punishment by the Almighty for this person who had the temerity to persecute the Teacher is described in the *Habakkuk Commentary:*

> *For the blood of men and violence to the earth, to the city and all who dwell in it:* this means the wicked priest, whom, for the wrong done to the teacher of righteousness and the men of his party, God delivered into the hand of his enemies, afflicting him with a destroying scourge, in bitterness of soul, because he acted wickedly against his elect.[2]

When the wicked priest was thus punished is not known; but it is probable that the Teacher and the group were banished and went to Damascus, whence, later, they migrated down the Jordan Valley to Qumran. Some have alleged from these passages and others that the wicked priest crucified the Teacher of Righteousness. It is altogether possible that he did meet such a violent death (perhaps at the hands of Alexander Jannaeus), but it is only one of many possibilities. Even if he were crucified, there never accrued to the event the tremendous meaning which surrounded the Christ-crucifixion.

While this persecution was in progress a complaint was lodged that no help had come from quarters from which it might have been expected:

> This means the house of Absalom and the men of their party, who kept silence at the chastisement of the teacher of righteousness, and did not help him against the man of the lie, who rejected the law in the midst of their whole congregation.[3]

At the moment of greatest need some religious group, possibly in Jerusalem, headed by a man named Absalom, failed to support the Teacher of Righteousness. The picture of persecution and banishment of the Teacher is quite clear.

What was his work, and what were his accomplishments for the sect? At the outset he was a teacher who was sent to the Essene group, which at the time had not found a real sense of direction. For a period of twenty years or more he served as their leader. They believed he was sent by God and had the capacity to interpret the mysteries of God's will, all of which had been especially revealed to him. In interpretation of Habakkuk this aspect of the Teacher of Righteousness is described:

> And as for what it says, *that he may run who reads it,* this means the teacher of righteousness, to whom God made known all the mysteries of the words of his servants the prophets.[4]

As previously indicated, the Essenes were expected to have

faith in the interpretation of Law made by the Teacher and in his personal integrity. Salvation came as the Law and prophets were explained and as men having learned the truth from the Teacher of Righteousness followed it scrupulously.

That this man was opposed to normative Judaism, and in his opposition was critical of many aspects of that faith, cannot be called in question. In this respect he stood in the great tradition of the prophets, as did Jesus.

So little is known about this shadowy figure that drawing a sketch of him, much less identifying him, is impossible. However, it is because of the infinitesimal amount of data which is in hand that writers have had free rein to let their imaginations go. Using Jesus as a model, some have reconstructed the Teacher of Righteousness and after finishing the job have announced an amazing resemblance between the two figures. Indeed, what could one expect!

Jesus was believed by the early Church to be the Risen Messiah who had submitted unto the death of the cross and had been raised by God from the dead. He was expected to return in glory. The Teacher of Righteousness was not the Messiah and there was not attached to his story any death-resurrection event such as Jesus experienced.

In their teachings there are, to be sure, parallels. Both were critical of the institutions and practices of Judaism, but so were all the prophets before them. Each, according to his own peculiar disposition, stood ideologically in the line of the prophets. There was, however, a major difference. With Jesus' criticism and that of the Church went the gentle invitation to become a part of the New Israel. Official Judaism rejected the Christian confrontation, with the result that the new faith was not accepted by Judaism as a whole. No such evangelistic attitude is manifest among the Essenes, who themselves rejected and broke with Judaism and were happy to have the breach become permanent.

Jesus and the Teacher of Righteousness were apparently both teachers *par excellence* whose followers felt that through them God had revealed the mysteries of His will. Essenism, to some extent, was founded upon the teachings of its master, whereas Christianity was based on the saving work of Christ more than on His teachings alone. There are countless other figures who share the teaching ministry with Jesus but few taught "as one having authority, and not as their scribes." (Matthew 7:29.)

Great capital has been made of the fact that both leaders were persecuted, but this serves only to make them a part of a great company of the spiritually loyal and brave in all ages. Any innovator will be persecuted, as Jeremiah and Amos both learned. John the Baptist and Paul felt the scourge and both went to death for their faith, but this hardly makes them eligible for identification with Jesus.

To sum up, it can be said with absolute accuracy that never have a few writers drawn so many conclusions from so little evidence as has been done in the comparisons of Jesus and the Teacher of Righteousness. In no sense at all was Jesus a late copy or reincarnation of the earlier model. To some extent both He and the Teacher of Righteousness bear a resemblance to the prophetic movement out of which each came. Since they lived in more or less contemporary periods and were faced with similar circumstances, that alone would provide an air of resemblance. The divergence in teaching, in attitude, and in saving work is so great, however, that one can but conclude that the two are as far apart as two spiritual leaders coming from the same culture, living in generally the same times, could be. The uniqueness and originality of

Jesus, far from being dimmed by the discovery of this Essene Teacher, have been greatly enhanced in contrast.

The air of the ancient Near East immediately before and during the life of Jesus was filled with Messianic expectation. Both the Church and Qumran lived in that atmosphere. But while Essenes waited for the advent of the Messiahs of Aaron and Israel, the Church welcomed Jesus as its Messiah. His spiritual Kingdom was established by the death-resurrection event, and His Church looked forward with confidence to His return with power. The Essene Teacher was the founder of his group who taught them to expect a Messiah, but he was not himself that Messiah. Resemblances between him and Jesus are incidental and should not be magnified out of proportion. The cosmic event of the Incarnation still stands solitary in the midst of history.

9. | *Influence and Coincidence*

THE ESSENES long ago vanished from this world, but still their influence on the development of the living Church constitutes a tantalizing study for the student of Christian origins. Except for this brief encounter with the Christian Church in its formative stages the study of Essenism would have interested only historians, linguists, and archaeologists, together with the more avid students of religion. In plain fact, however, the Essene religious group at Qumran fills a gap in our knowledge of an era in the development of Hebrew religious thought about which little has previously been known. Samples of the language (Aramaic) which Jesus spoke may now be read from the so-called Dead Sea Scrolls—a matter of supreme importance to the understanding of some New Testament texts. Moreover, the whole inner struggle of Jew against Jew in the post-Maccabean period up to the Christian age can now be traced. Words and ideas have come to life once more and their meanings have been made clear, thus helping the reader to know meanings not superimposed by a modern commentator but intended by the ancient writer.

Summing up a treatment such as this is not simple because the evidence often allows for honest difference of opinion among competent scholars. With that in mind and with the sure knowledge that tomorrow's new finds may alter these conclusions, the results of this study are presented under five brief headings.

Direct Influence

Exactly how direct contact between the early Church and Qumran was made cannot be determined, but it is certain that the leaders of the Christian movement were aware of the Essene sect and knew its general principles. The writer is of the opinion that John the Baptist, the author of John's Gospel, and the Apostle Paul had some direct contact with the Essene group resident at Khirbet Qumran. It may be that Paul's only contact was ideological, through reading the writings of this sect; but not so with the other two, whose knowledge is too detailed to allow for such impersonal contacts only.

The form of the Lord's Supper and of baptism were in all probability borrowed by Christianity from Qumran even though their content and method of administration were almost immediately changed. Baptism became an initiatory, unrepeatable ceremony for the Church, while the meaning of the sacramental meal developed along utterly different lines from that in vogue with the Qumran sect. Not only was there an anticipatory aspect to the Christian symbolic meal, it was also transformed into a memorial feast honoring the Messiah's finished work in the death-resurrection event. The death-resurrection symbolism which Paul employed is also unique with Christianity. Form was borrowed by the church but the content of faith was added as the Christian movement articulated its own distinctive theological position.

In addition to these influences, which we call direct for want of a more indistinct term, there is obviously some very direct imprint of Essenism on the orientation for prayer among early Christians as well as the orientation of ancient church buildings toward the east. This could hardly be coincidental. How the influence was mediated, or through whom, cannot be finally determined on the basis of present evidence.

The area of greatest influence is the light-darkness motif expressed in both Christianity and Essenism in practically identical terms. After many guesses concerning the exact meaning of the dualistic point of view in the New Testament, that definition and background have now been discovered in the Qumran literature. The mediating position between Zoroastrianism and the New Testament can definitely be assigned to the Essenes. To be sure, the development of the idea of struggle, its meaning in history, and its consummation are not the same with the two communities. But if Christianity borrowed from Qumran at all, the evidence at this point is most abundant.

Direct influence was limited to the matters of the sacraments, the orientation for prayer and building, and the light-darkness motif. Good evidence exists for these conclusions but no such strong case can be developed at this time for other alleged influences.

Indirect or Coincidental Influence

In this category must be listed the parallel approach to treatment of an offending brother in the two communities and the use of twelve as a key to both organizations. Also descriptions of both good and evil persons may have some indirect connection. Resemblances between the Essene Teacher of Righteousness and Jesus are coincidental and are to be explained by the fact that both leaders came out of a prophetic background and each founded a movement. The two men separately left a tremendous imprint on their respective groups but the matter of identification is out of the question, and real similarity is unlikely.

Most important among the coincidental influences is separation from the world which each group claimed but with different meanings. Esoteric truth was a thing to be protected by the Essenes but truth was to be shared by Christians with all who had the eyes of faith. The Church withdrew from the world that the world might emulate the new society and become a part of it, whereas Qumran had no such desire or mission.

In the matter of giving up private property in the two communities the connection is at most coincidental, with no common origin or influence of one group upon the other. Reason, motivation, and development in Qumran and within the Church, so far as this facet of common life went, were completely at variance.

Background in Common

The major proportion of contacts, influences, and similarities which have been adduced by various writers comparing Qumran on the one hand and the Church on the other must be placed in the category of a common background. Emphasis on the sovereignty of God, the care with which Scripture was treated, and recognition of the creative power of the Almighty are patently drawn from the common background of Hebrew faith and Judaism.

The sense of an impending consummation of the age, with God judging the unrighteous, was original with neither group but comes rather from a common source which had become an atmosphere of the times. Messianic concepts are the heritage of ancient Israel and its literature, not of either of these later developments. Similarities in Messianic content are to be explained in this way, whereas divergences are the result of basic differences within the two movements. Essenism expected Messiahs who would be preceded by a prophet; but, unlike Christianity, the Qumran enclave had yet to recognize the presence of the Messiah in their midst.

As has been pointed out in several places, appearance of a marked influence of the Teacher of Righteousness on Jesus is wholly imaginary. However, the two men do possibly share characteristics which would inevitably result from the common heritage.

Differences

No attempt is made here to list the marked differences in degree and in kind between the two religious movements. Salvation by faith is at the top of the list, followed closely by doctrines of the Incarnation and of the Trinity. In attitude Christianity looked outward with a great commission to fulfill, while Qumran, secure in the desert, was introspective, guarding its secrets to the death. One movement was zealously missionary while the other was ingrown.

In the matter of law the two could hardly have been further apart. At Qumran stringent external rules were applied to each area of living, while Jesus got to the heart of the matter—motivation. Whatever tendency there was in Christianity to return officially to legalism was dealt a deathblow by the work of Paul, whose personal experience dictated his attitude.

Naturally the close-knit community at Qumran developed a more rigid organization, having in it a sense of rank and decorum such as came later in some phases of the Church's history, but not in all of it. The movement of Christ fanned out across the world with a quasi-democratic feeling among its members, who all having been made equal in Christ allowed no sense of rank.

Suffice it to say in conclusion that the two movements are about as different as they could have been, given the fact that both came out of a common cultural and historical background. There were some cross-influences but not many. Both were distinctive outgrowths of the Hebrew faith, from which each emerged with a different emphasis. With every new development the divergences became more marked.

Values

At this point the reader might well feel more confused than he did when he began this volume and might be led to ask, "Why all the noise if the influence of the Qumran sect on the origins of Christianity is no greater than here described?" Although this attitude is understandable, we should not depreciate the new knowledge and evidence which the Dead Sea Scrolls afford, since this evidence still bids fair to revolutionize various phases of New Testament studies.

The era in which the Christian Church originated and developed is better known since these archaeological discoveries were made. In fact, a blank spot in the immediate pre-Christian and contemporary history of events and ideas can be partially filled. Like the discovery of a few lost pieces of a jig-saw puzzle, this evidence makes possible the fitting together of many other independent parts into an intelligible whole. Furthermore, manifold elusive thought patterns (e.g., light-darkness) come through now with greater force than they did previous to 1948.

In addition to these not inconsiderable values, another sect of Judaism can now be added to the well-known Sadducee and Pharisee parties. Although the existence of the Essenes was known from several sources, no intimate knowledge of the inner workings of the group was actually in hand. Through the windows which these scrolls have opened we can see clearly the agitated state of flux which Judaism was experiencing just prior to the coming of Jesus Christ. No static era this, but one in which the hopes and fears of people had come to a great climax, with several general courses of action being taken by various religious factions.

The figure, the work, and the teachings of Jesus stand out in bold contrast against the picture of Essene faith developed from the Qumran material. Saving grace and love for all men are concepts still so grand as to stagger the imagination. Incarnation and resurrection are even more glorious than before. The knowledge of victory in Christ, communion with His presence, and promise of a new Kingdom are mightier now than before.

In the light of the Dead Sea Scrolls, the living Church examines with new insight its historical origins while rejoicing in the unique revelation which is in Christ Jesus. Christians have already experienced that victory of faith which is their possession, a triumph the holy men in the desert dimly saw but never reached. The living Church is alive because it was essentially different at the beginning from the Essene sect, which has perished from the earth. Moreover, the Master of the Church Himself embodied and wrought out in life the eternal "good news" which has redeemed the lives of men throughout the ages. To this living faith the believer can give himself with new confidence, in the sure knowledge that Jesus is still "the way, and the truth, and the life."

Notes and Acknowledgments

Chapter 1 • The Desert Speaks

1. Cf. Millar Burrows, *The Dead Sea Scrolls*, p. 382.
2. From *The Dead Sea Scrolls* by Millar Burrows, p. 359. Copyright 1955 by Millar Burrows. Reprinted by permission of The Viking Press, Inc., New York.
3. *Ibid.*, p. 414.
4. *Ibid.*, p. 378.
5. Joshua 1:8. (Scripture quotations are from the American Standard Version, copyright, 1929, by International Council of Religious Education.)
6. Cf. Psalm 1:2.
7. Condensed from Millar Burrows, *op. cit.*, pp. 380-381.
8. Millar Burrows, *op. cit.*, p. 360.

Chapter 3 • John the Baptist and the Essenes

1. Luke 1:80.
2. Carl H. Kraeling, *John the Baptist*, pp. 35-36. Charles Scribner's Sons, New York, 1951. (Arrangement slightly adapted.) Used by permission.

Chapter 4 • Sacraments and Worship

1. Arranged from John 13:6-10.
2. Frank M. Cross, "Qumran Cave I" (a review of *Qumran Cave I: Discoveries in the Judaean Desert, I*, by D. Barthélemy and J. T. Milik, Oxford, 1955), in *Journal of Biblical Literature*, June 1956 (Vol. LXXV, Part II, pp. 124-125). Used by permission. (The bracketed paragraph is a correction in translation made by Dr. Cross. In the other paragraphs translated by Dr. Cross, from page 117 of *Discoveries*

in the Judaean Desert, interior brackets indicating the fragmentary nature of the material have been omitted.)

Chapter 5 • Organization and Nature of the Two Communities

1. Arranged from Acts 1:6-7.
2. Millar Burrows, *The Dead Sea Scrolls,* p. 381.
3. *Ibid.,* p. 371.
4. *Ibid.,* p. 379.
5. *Ibid.,* p. 378.
6. *Ibid.,* p. 373.
7. *Ibid.,* p. 378.
8. *Ibid.*

Chapter 6 • From Darkness to Light

1. Millar Burrows, *The Dead Sea Scrolls,* p. 374.
2. *Ibid.,* p. 375.
3. *Ibid.,* p. 376.
4. See Karl Georg Kuhn, "New Light on Temptation, Sin, and Flesh in the New Testament," in *The Scrolls and the New Testament,* edited by Krister Stendahl, pp. 94-113. Harper & Brothers, 1957. By permission.
5. Burrows, *op cit.,* p. 375
6. *Ibid.*

Chapter 7 • Creeds in Common?

1. Millar Burrows, *The Dead Sea Scrolls,* p. 407.
2. *Ibid.,* p. 368.
3. *Ibid.,* p. 388.
4. *Ibid.,* p. 413.
5. *Ibid.,* pp. 367-368.
6. *Ibid.,* p. 412.

Chapter 8 • The Messiahs, the Teacher of Righteousness, and Jesus

1. Millar Burrows, *The Dead Sea Scrolls,* pp. 369-370.
2. *Ibid.,* p. 369.
3. *Ibid.,* p. 367.
4. *Ibid.,* p. 368.

Selected Bibliography in English

Allegro, J. M., *The Dead Sea Scrolls*. London: Penguin Books, 1956.

Avigad, Nahmen, and Yadin, Yigael, *A Genesis Apocryphon*. Jerusalem: The Magnes Press, 1956.

Bruce, F. F., *Second Thoughts on the Dead Sea Scrolls*. Grand Rapids: Wm. B. Eerdmans Publishing Company, 1956.

Bruce, F. F., *The Teacher of Righteousness in the Qumran Texts*. London: Tyndale Press, 1957.

Burrows, Millar, *The Dead Sea Scrolls*. New York: The Viking Press, 1956.

Cross, Frank M., Jr., "The Dead Sea Scrolls" in *The Interpreter's Bible*, Vol. XII, pp. 645-667. New York: Abingdon Press, 1957.

Dupont-Sommer, A., *The Dead Sea Scrolls*. Oxford: Basil Blackwell & Mott, Ltd.; New York: The Macmillan Company, 1952.

Dupont-Sommer, A., *The Jewish Sect of Qumran and the Essenes*. London: Vallentine, Mitchell & Company, Ltd., 1954.

Davies, A. Powell, *The Meaning of the Dead Sea Scrolls*. New York: The New American Library of World Literature, Inc., 1956.

Fritsch, Charles T., *The Qumran Community*. New York: The Macmillan Company, 1956.

Gaster, Theodor H., *The Dead Sea Scriptures*. New York: Doubleday & Company, Inc., 1956.

Graystone, Geoffrey, S. M., *The Dead Sea Scrolls and the Originality of Christ*. New York: Sheed & Ward, Inc., 1956.

Murphy, Roland E., *The Dead Sea Scrolls and the Bible*. Westminster, Md.: Newman Press, 1956.

Rowley, H. H., *Jewish Apocalyptic and the Dead Sea Scrolls*. London: The Athlone Press, 1957.

Rowley, H. H., *The Zadokite Fragments and the Dead Sea Scrolls*. Oxford: Basil Blackwell & Mott, Ltd., 1952; New York: The Macmillan Company, 1953.

Schoenfield, Hugh J., *Secrets of the Dead Sea Scrolls*. London: Vallentine, Mitchell & Company, Ltd., 1956.

Stendahl, Krister, Editor, *The Scrolls and the New Testament*. New York: Harper & Brothers, 1957.

Vermes, Geza, *Discovery in the Judean Desert*. New York: Desclee Company, 1956.

Wilson, Edmund, *The Scrolls from the Dead Sea*. London: Oxford University Press, 1955.

Index of Scripture

Index of Subjects

Aaron, Messiah of, 101-102, 108
Absalom, 105
Aenon, trading post, 47, 49, 50
Agape feast, 58-59
Ain Feshka, 22, 23, 24, 26, 27
Akeldama, burial place of Judas, 66
Alexander Jannaeus, 19, 34, 105
Alexander the Great, 17-18
Amman, Jordan, museum, 41
Amos, prophet, 107
Ananias, 72
Antiochus Epiphanes, 18
Apocrypha and apocryphal books: Enoch, 79; found among scrolls, 43; Jubilees, 79; Twelve Patriarchs, 79
Apostles. *See* Church organization; James; John; Paul; Peter
Aramaic, language of Jesus, 109
Aristobulus I, 19
Armageddon, 37
Avigad, Nahmen, 43

Babylonian Exile. *See* Exile, Babylonian
Baptism: as a burial ceremony, 55; as rite of initiation, 50, 52, 54; by John the Baptist, 49-50, 52, 54; connection with Qum-

ran, 110; early Church practice, 52, 54-55, 64; form, 54-55
Barsabbas, 66
Bath, Ritual, 27-28, 33, 52, 54
Bedouins, 15, 21, 22, 23
Bethabara. *See* Bethany beyond the Jordan
Bethany beyond the Jordan, 47, 50
Bethlehem, 16, 34
Bible: books found in Dead Sea caves, 43. *See also* books of the Bible by name
Bishop, officer of the church, 31, 68-69
Brownlee, William, 46
Burrows, Millar, 41; translation of scrolls quoted, 28, 29, 36, 67-68, 70-71, 75, 76, 77, 80-81, 81-82, 88, 91, 92, 93, 95, 97, 99, 104, 105

Cairo *genizah*, 27, 42
Caves. *See* Dead Sea Scrolls
Celibacy, 32
Church, Early: attitude toward offending brother, 75-76, 78, 111; attitude toward property ownership, 70-72, 77, 112; attitude toward world, 73-75, 78,